from page to stage

from page to stage

inspiration, tools, and
public speaking tips for writers

Betsy Graziani Fasbinder

SHE WRITES PRESS

Published August 7, 2018
Printed in the United States of America
Print ISBN: 978-1-63152-463-9
E-ISBN: 978-1-63152-464-6
Library of Congress Control Number: 2018942234

Cover and interior design by Tabitha Lahr

For information, address:
She Writes Press
1563 Solano Ave #546
Berkeley, CA 94707

She Writes Press is a division of SparkPoint Studio, LLC.

This book is dedicated to storytellers, past and present. You turn ink and breath and voice into entire worlds; I am in awe.

It is our stories that make us uniquely human, and sharing those stories in every art form that connects us most intimately to one another. I believe that it is through storytelling that we can bridge the deepest divides between people, connect to one another through compassion and empathy, and create the possibilities for understanding and peace.

My gratitude for stories and those who tell them is beyond measure.

A note to the grammarians of the world

In this book, it is my goal to provide a coach's voice to writers struggling to find the same courage in speaking as they find in their writing. I write here with an intentionally informal, conversational tone and have taken some liberties with the rules of grammar and punctuation to that end. I opt to vary my use of male/female pronouns to be inclusive, rather than always defaulting to one or the other. The skills and ideas taught here are valuable to anyone, of any gender identification. I hope you'll appreciate the liberties taken due to my intention of serving the book's ultimate purpose.

Contents

PART 3: HOW TO SAY IT: STAND AND DELIVER WITH SIMPLE SKILLS THAT MAKE ALL THE DIFFERENCE

PART 4: TRANSFORM PRESENTATIONS INTO CONVERSATIONS

PART 5: ADD THE BLING: TOUCHES THAT MAKE A TALK MEMORABLE

An Invitation to Every Writer

"There is no greater agony than bearing an untold story inside you."
—Maya Angelou, Author/Poet

You're a writer: published or not, a bestseller or indie. You've spent years, perhaps decades, writing draft after draft of your works. You take classes, go to conferences, pay dues to writing groups and organizations, and hire coaches, all to hone your craft. You agonize over your stories, excavate your expertise, imagination, and experiences—sometimes painful ones—to create a collection of poetry, a novel, a nonfiction book, or a memoir. You spend hours in libraries and online doing research. But it doesn't stop there.

Once your book is written, you'll likely pay editors and proofreaders to make it publish-ready. You may hunt for an agent or self-publish, in which case you'll need a cover designer and an interior designer. Then, you'll either DIY or hire a publicist, a website designer, and a social media expert to help build your promotional platform.

After all of that effort, expense, and anguish, you might still sabotage your writing's best chance at success.

But I'd never do that! you cry.

In fact, I meet authors and aspiring authors all the time—many with beautiful books and extraordinary stories to tell—who do exactly that. How? They sabotage their book's success by either avoiding opportunities to speak in public (out of fear or lack of confidence) or they don't prepare themselves to do it well and they squander the opportunities that they've created by white-knuckling it through a talk or an interview. They spent huge effort building their promotional platform, but forgot that the author herself is the best book promotion tool there is. *Ahem.* That'd be you.

Lots of people look at a skilled public speaker and think, *I wish I could do that. I wish I could speak with such confidence. I wish I could be so engaging, dynamic, and fascinating. I wish I'd gotten that gift.* Here's a little secret that I've learned, first for myself and then through teaching and coaching literally thousands of reluctant speakers: *Skilled public speaking is not a gift, but a set of simple, learnable skills that anyone willing to put in the effort can learn.*

Just like writing well, public speaking is a set of skills, techniques, and practices. Sure, the skills come more naturally to some than to others, but anyone can improve his speaking skills. Poor public speakers can gain skills and become proficient. Proficient speakers can become polished. Polished speakers can hone the art and become stars. I've seen it hundreds of times, and from the most unlikely speakers you'd ever imagine. Your book and your ideas deserve the best, most skilled ambassador to share them, and that, dear writer, is you.

Why I Wrote This Book

"My morality was formed because booksellers put certain books in my way. We owe them and authors a great debt."
—Gabriel Tallent, author, *My Absolute Darling*

I'm a lifelong reader and writer, turned author in 2013. As I heard Gabriel Tallent express his gratitude in the words above at his book launch event in my community, I was reminded of how much books, booksellers, and authors have meant to me throughout my life. I want to be a champion for the voices of creative people, particularly writers—my tribe.

Finding your speaking voice and making it as powerful and unique as your writing voice will help you publish and promote your book and your ideas. That means your stories will find their way into a broader world and give you a wider exposure. Whatever your purpose in writing stories, that purpose will be more possible if you can speak well in public.

I want to spare you the agony so many writers suffer. I want to offer you tools and inspiration to speak with authority, confidence, authenticity, and impact. You deserve it. Your book deserves it.

The world needs your voice—lofty, but true. I'm not the only one who thinks so.

"Done right, a talk can electrify a room and transform an audience's worldview. Done right, a talk is more powerful than anything in written form. Writing gives us words. Speaking brings with it a whole new toolbox."
—Chris Anderson, Head of TED, *TED Talks*

How to Use This Book to Maximum Effect

"I like a teacher who gives you something to take home to think about besides homework."
—Lily Tomlin, comedian

Through this book I'll offer plenty of examples, usable tools and techniques, and a whole lot of cheering for your efforts. Some of these you can apply instantly and see changes right away. Others require more practice and take more time to learn. In addition to the tools and techniques, I'll offer other recurring features to help you along:

Quotes. Lots of quotes: I am inspired by beautifully crafted words and use them as inspiration sources, so I'm sharing lots of those with you. I hope they'll inspire you, too.

Mental Shifts. While many of the techniques and tools we need for skilled public speaking are of the "how to" variety (which I'll cover extensively), the biggest barrier to skilled public speaking is often in our thinking and our assumptions. I'll offer Mental Shifts throughout the book to invite you to expand your thinking, challenge what you assume, and welcome new ideas about speaking with confidence and skill.

Make It Stick Segments. Because we all learn in different ways, I'll offer suggestions for video, audio, TV, and radio examples as well as writing exercises that help make the concepts more vivid and give you a chance to see them in practice. Most are fun, some require reflection, others require you to stretch and take risks in order to grow.

In order to get the most out of this book, I'm going to ask a few things of you. I ask you to be open: mind, body, and spirit. Be open to shifting some of your assumptions and attitudes about yourself and about your ability to speak well to an audience of any size. If you simply read this book and welcome some pretty enthusiastic cheerleading on my part, I'm confident you'll gather some tips, tricks, and tools that will help you to hone your skills. If you go deeper and *actually do* the exercises I offer, I predict your learning will be deeper and more lasting. View and listen to as many of the video and audio resources as you can, and take notice of events you witness on TV, radio, online, or in person. This type of learning—developing skills to speak with skill and confidence—is a process, not a single event. Speaking well, like writing or any other art form, is a lifelong learning process.

A bonus side effect of learning these skills is that you'll become a more astute consumer of spoken presentations. You'll start discerning what works when a speaker talks and, just as importantly, what doesn't work. Whether you're watching writers, teachers, members of the clergy, comedians, politicians, or late-night TV infomercials, you can learn by watching with a discerning eye. Rather than "liking" or "not liking" speakers as a reflex response, you'll be able to identify what you're responding to in their style. Just as reading great books and terrible ones teaches us how to write, watching great and terrible talks will teach us how to speak in public.

Why You Can Trust Me . . . and a Confession

If you're going to learn from someone, you should probably know a bit about her background.

I am a writer and have been all my life—or at least since I could write. I've ghostwritten one published book and this is the third book of my own to date. I have also been a licensed psychotherapist for more than twenty-five years, so I know a bit about anxiety, its sources, and how to manage it. I've provided professional public speaking coaching and training to the hesitant, the downright phobic, and the falsely confident (rare, but occasional) since 1998 and have worked in Fortune 500 companies, start-ups, and nonprofit organizations across the U.S. and abroad, both for my own business and as a trainer for other companies, working at every level of organizations from executives to new-hires. I'm fortunate to have worked for training companies that charge an impressive amount of money for my services to companies who are glad to pay it, and do so repeatedly. They know the value of having their leaders and team members skilled to communicate their ideas. My client list also includes writers, artists, and entrepreneurs, with a few politicians thrown in the mix.

While all of the above are relevant as credentials for writing this book, what might be most relevant to you if you're at all apprehensive about public speaking (or if the thought of it horrifies you) is that I suffered with *glossophobia* well into my late thirties, though few others in my life were aware of it at the time. *Glossophobia* is a profound fear of public speaking. The term comes from the Greek words *glossa,* meaning tongue, and *phobos*, meaning fear or dread. (Which sounds like fear of tongues, but maybe that's just me.) Glossophobia is one the most common of all fears but, in its extreme forms, it's no joke.

"I have big, big stage fright."
—Andrea Bocelli, internationally renowned opera singer

Who knew I had something in common with Andrea Bocelli? Perhaps you do, too.

As a kid and well into my college and graduate school years, if I was called on in class, when all eyes turned on me I thought I was going to be ill. My ears got hot. Sweat trickled down my spine. My guts went to jelly. I felt the heat of blotchy hives climbing from my chest to my throat. Even if I knew the answer, I'd freeze and say nothing (in elementary and high school), and often had to fight back tears. Being *looked at* felt that intense, though I learned to mask it. Teachers soon learned not to call on me—some out of frustration, others out of mercy. Into adulthood, I'd be sick before job interviews and suffer anxiety and sleeplessness for weeks before I had to make a presentation or do a training at work. While I've always been verbal and communicated comfortably in a one-on-one or small group setting, it was not until late in my thirties that I addressed and largely conquered my biggest fears of public speaking. I did so by learning and practicing the simple skills and modified tools I'll share with you here in this book.

I still get nervous sometimes when the stakes are high or when the topic is new. (I consider myself a recovering glossophobe. One day at a time.) But today I have the skills to manage those nerves and deliver the messages I want to deliver in the way I want to deliver them. Today, a fear of speaking no longer keeps me from doing anything I want to do.

This can be true for you, too.

Start by Giving Your Thinking a Good Scrub

"Your assumptions are your windows on the world. Scrub them off every once in a while, or the light won't come in."
—Isaac Asimov, author, professor of biochemistry

Perhaps you are holding assumptions about whether you do can do public speaking well, or even have the potential to do it well. I ask that you take the advice of Isaac Asimov in the quote above; scrub those assumptions off. The skills of good public speaking can be learned. The tools can be utilized. It's not rocket science. The biggest obstacles for most potentially fabulous and inspiring speakers are the attitudes and assumptions they hold, and the lack of a few simple skills they can develop when willing.

I coached one author to help her prepare for her book launch. She wrote a stunning book. In the first moments of our time together, she boldly announced, "I know that I'll never be one of those WOW kind of dynamic, charismatic public speakers. I just want you to help me to get through my book launch without humiliating myself."

Doesn't "not humiliating yourself" seem like a pretty low bar? Have you adopted a similar limiting belief about yourself and your capabilities that keeps you from even beginning to gain the skills to actually *be* dynamic, engaging, amusing, entertaining, informative, and inspiring?

What self-limiting beliefs do you hold about yourself as a speaker? I propose that these beliefs may or, more likely, may not be accurate. What's more, even if they've been accurate in the past, they do not have to be so going forward.

By the way, that client of mine with the low bar—she was a WOW at her book launch after learning a few simple skills.

Breathe

"It's never too late to be what you might have been."
—George Eliot, author

Here's my invitation: As you read this book and do the exercises, I invite you to set your resistance aside and let your freak-out muscles relax. *Ahh.* There.

If you're a hopeful or newbie author or a highly nervous speaker, there's something in this book for you. If you're an experienced speaker or a natural extrovert, there's a lot here for you, too. My hope is that one of the mind-shifting ideas or simple skills that I'll describe will be that just-at-the-right-time nugget to inspire your confidence, and that the practical take-away skills will help you look and feel more polished. My sincerest hope is that you'll get lots of nuggets.

I invite you to use these pages as your personal cheerleader, helping to inspire you to invest in yourself as the most important part of your book-promoting platform. I also invite you to connect with me via my website or my Facebook author page, which are listed in the resources in the Bonus Track chapter at the end of the book. Let me know what you think, ask me questions, tell me how you're doing. I always like to know how the story progresses.

While I'm addressing writers and authors in these pages, the principles are applicable to any artist, musician, entrepreneur, or, indeed, anyone who wants to speak more effectively and confidently about his creative endeavors. Practicing a creative art and talking about that art are two different skills—both are invaluable.

What This Book Is *Not*

As much as I love books, not everything can be learned from reading alone. Someone could read a million pages about playing the piano, dancing ballet, or how to execute a perfect golf swing and still not be able to play Chopin, dance *Swan Lake*, or make a great drive down a fairway.

Public speaking skills are more akin to musical or athletic skills than intellectual knowledge alone. Mastery does not take place simply in your brain; it takes place in your body, in the "doing" of it. This book is not intended to replace the practice and live coaching for those who can benefit from it—which is anyone, really.

I always advise getting some live, in-the-room coaching if you can. If private coaching or professional classes aren't an option for you, either because of cost or your location, consider Toastmasters. Toastmasters is a fabulous international organization with membership available for a nominal annual fee. Some workplaces sponsor membership for their employees. It's is a great place to get support, encouragement, practice, and coaching in a low-stakes environment.

If you prefer (or need) private coaching, finding a good coach is important. If you have a friend who can recommend someone, great. Or check with your local Toastmasters chapter. They likely have local referrals, some from within their organization. New technology has made private coaching via videoconference another possibility. I've coached people via the telephone for years. Today coaches like myself can coach people in any geography using videoconference technology. It's not quite the same as being there in person, but it's pretty darned close.

What This Book Is

"The future belongs to those who believe in the beauty of their dreams."
—Eleanor Roosevelt, politician, activist, First Lady of the United States

I'm a shameless writer-event junkie. Many of these are amazing, inspiring experiences by authors who have honed their speaking skills along with their writing craft. When I attend events featuring new authors or those whose work I've long admired, only to see them fearful and struggling—so overwhelmed by their fear that they looked more as though they were suffering than celebrating—it fills me with sadness. Speaking doesn't have to be so miserable.

It really doesn't.

I also attend events where the writer may not be obviously fearful, but he has habits or mannerisms that either distract from or contradict his message. This also seems a sad shame. With only a little coaching, a few tweaks, and some practice, these pesky problems can be eliminated so that the author and his work can shine.

Stretch to Get Warmed Up

Athletes always do some stretching before they begin a strenuous fitness activity. Given that I'm asking you to build some new strengths, it makes sense that we should start with a stretch. Let's start our first Mental Shift and a Make It Stick exercise.

MENTAL SHIFT

You can grow to have fun speaking in public?

If you'd offered me this mental shift in 1997, the roar of my laughter would have blown you out of the room. (Well, maybe not a roar; I am an introvert, after all.) I know this today: not only is it possible for nearly anyone to become a skilled public speaker, it's also possible to become much more than that—a person who enjoys sharing your ideas with groups of people assembled to hear them. You can gain the skills, change your experience as a speaker, and actually have a good time.

Come on. Let that thinking percolate. Imagine yourself at the front of your favorite bookstore surrounded by interested readers. Imagine yourself and your ideas making a difference—entertaining, inspiring, educating, amusing, enlightening. Imagine yourself having fun! Walt Disney said, "If you can dream it, you can do it."

I invite you to start dreaming.

Make It Stick

In each of the Making It Stick exercises, I'll provide suggested titles of talks and podcasts. Because URLs change and links die, I suggest doing a Google search by title for each suggested link.

 EXERCISE #1: REFLECTION
Please write your *thoughtful* answers to the following. No . . . really write them. There's learning to be had:

1. When you attend or view a writer event as an audience member, what do you look for from the experience?
2. Describe the best writer event you've attended. What elements made it so?
3. Describe the worst writer event you've attended. What elements made it so?

4. Can you think of any way that fear or lack of confidence has kept you from writing or from promoting your writing?

5. If you could be assured that you'd do it well, what would be your DREAM speaking event?

6. Start a "nugget" list of the insights you gain from reading this book, doing the exercises, and observing the videos, interviews, and other media moments I provide, or those you find on your own. Use a paper or electronic notebook to do the exercises and to make notes about what you observe when you follow the links I provide. Also make note of what you begin to notice in everyday life, at in-person events, or during media presentations you consume.

 ### EXERCISE #2: VIEW J.P. SEARS'S TED TALK, "SAYING YES! TO YOUR WEIRDNESS"

Sears is ridiculous and fun and his comedic videos are deliciously irreverent. Consider yourself warned. Still, there's something to be learned from this inspiring clown.

Use your notebook to record the following:

1. What "nugget" of information or inspiration did you gain from the talk?

2. What delivery style did you notice in J.P. Sears? What did you like about his delivery? What didn't you like?

 ### EXERCISE #3: VIEW LIDIA YUKNAVITCH'S TED TALK "THE BEAUTY OF BEING A MISFIT"

1. In what way might you be a misfit?

2. How has being a misfit helped you? Hindered you?

3. What "nugget" did you gain from Lidia's talk?

4. What did you notice about her style?

PART 1

It's an Inside Job: Getting Your Heart and Mind Ready for Speaking

"Being able to read well in public and talk about your work in an engaging fashion is part of most writers' job specifications."
—Sara Sheridan, author

Why This Information Comes First

When our younger son was about ten, my husband and I were preparing to paint our family room. "I want to help," our son said with a gleeful look on his face, spinning a clean paint roller. "Sure," my husband said. "First we have to organize all of our equipment to make sure we have everything, then we scrub the walls, fill the holes, and tape off all of the windows." Our son practically wilted. Then he quickly dropped the roller and booked it to his buddy's house. Smart boy. The prep work wasn't as exciting as rolling paint on the walls, but it was necessary to make the next part of the work go faster and to get the desired result.

The same is true for developing skills as a speaker. When I coach people, their first urge is to dive into their content, or start making PowerPoint slides, or write a script for their remarks. (Many brands of presentation software exist, though PowerPoint is the most common. Like "Kleenex" and "Band-Aid," some brands become the description of all brands. I'll use this branded term to mean any presentation software.)

Before we get to content and delivery, some important and invisible *internal* prep work makes the design and delivery of our talks go more smoothly.

That's what part 1 is about: the invisible, internal prep work that will make the skill development happen more smoothly: the inside job. Let part 1 be your cheerleader and your champion. We all need that now and then. Part 1 is not about "how" to speak, but *why*, and why you are the perfect person to speak about your writing. Think of this section as the primer coat; the color will go on a whole lot easier if you start here.

I invite you to go through part 1 with an open heart. By doing this internal work, and later adding the skills and techniques offered in parts 2 and 3, you'll have much of what you need to speak with skill, authenticity, and passion to audiences of any size, about topics of your choosing.

"There is no passion to be found playing it small—in settling for life that is less than the one you are capable of living."
—Nelson Mandela, revolutionary, president of South Africa

Here I'd like to give you the biggest spoiler for the whole topic of public speaking, right here in the first pages. *You are already a skilled public speaker.* No, wait. Don't close the book. You are. Let me clarify here what I mean by "public" speaking by offering another of the many "mental shifts" that I'll invite you to make throughout this book.

MENTAL SHIFT

If you've ever gotten a job, talked someone into something, or advocated for a loved one's needs, YOU are already a skilled "public" speaker.
Whenever you're talking to other humans, you ARE a public speaker. The skills required to talk in a job interview, when influencing a friend, or negotiating with family members are the precise skills you need for public speaking.

When writers think of public speaking, they're usually envisioning a huge crowd of people with their eyes glued to the front of the room where the writer stands. We should all be so lucky to have a large group come to hear about our books. I wish that for every writer. This formal kind of presentation is just one of the many public speaking opportunities you'll have as a writer and as a published author, but it's not the most frequent one by far. Here are just a few:

- Book launches
- Agent/editor/publisher pitches (in person)

- Reading your work aloud
- Moderating panels, hosting events
- Being a panelist
- Conducting workshops and classes
- Media interviews (radio, podcasts, and TV)
- Talks with booksellers, asking them to stock your book or host an event
- Service group and writers' group addresses
- Cocktail party talk (by which I mean any time you're at an informal gathering and someone asks, "So, what are you writing about?")
- Keynote addresses and other inspirational speaking
- Creating a podcast
- Speaking on a book trailer
- TED Talks
- Trade shows, county fairs, farmers' markets
- Facebook Live events

All of these (and more) are public speaking. Some require preparation while others are impromptu. I invite you to start noticing yourself in your personal and informal environments. Notice when you capture attention. Notice when you entertain. Notice when others are intrigued by what you're talking about. Yeah, you. *That* public speaker. I want to bring that *you* to the front of the room. I want that *you* to show up at your own book launch and slay it, and have a blast, and sell lots of books.

Getting that natural you, your most captivating and comfortable self, to show up for every kind of presentation—formal or casual, prepared or impromptu, large group or one-on-one—is the entire purpose of this book.

In Part 1, we'll cover:
- The fear factors of public speaking and inspirations for quelling them
- Some assumptions we hold that can get in the way of our speaking skills
- Mental shifts we can make to approach speaking without assumptions or attitudes that hinder us
- The rewards, both measurable and intangible, for learning to speak with passion, confidence, and authenticity to audiences of any size

Let's get started.

CHAPTER 1

What's Sooooooo Scary about Public Speaking?

"There are two types of speakers in the world: the nervous ones and the liars."
—Mark Twain, author

Fear of public speaking can range from a minor annoyance to full-blown, paralyzing terror. Though by saying so I'm at risk of minimizing my work as a therapist, simply understanding *why* we get nervous about public speaking doesn't change the fact that we do. Still, it's useful to name our fears so that we can examine and overcome them by learning some skills and changing our mindset.

Most people's fears of public speaking fall into a few categories:

Fear of Looking the Fool

"To be honest, I'm normally proudest of myself after I do something that frightens me."
—J.K. Rowling, author of the *Harry Potter* series

Over and over again my coaching clients say things like, "I just don't want to look foolish."

For many of us, the simple fear is this: *I just don't want to feel embarrassed in front of a group of people.* This fear may come from our past experiences of feeling embarrassed, being made fun of, or even being ridiculed. Those who've had such experiences deserve support and empathy, of course. You also deserve to have your own confident voice, even if you've had such experiences.

Can there be embarrassing moments in public speaking? Sure! I've had my share—perhaps more than my share. I did a pratfall of epic proportion in front of a group of more than a hundred. At an outdoor venue, a seagull, with great conspicuous spectacle, pooped on my microphone just as I began to address a group. Heck, I even started one presentation in the wrong ballroom at a conference (signage problem) and had to zip into the next room and start over. And still, I'm here to tell the tale. By the way, I was invited back to that conference with the bad signage the following year because people gave me high scores for my session, commenting especially about how much fun I made of the error.

I will not promise you that you won't ever feel embarrassed in front of a group. I will offer you ways to make that a pink-faced moment rather than a down-to-the-core public humiliation. And, you can use those pink-faced moments to your advantage. For that you'll need a safety net. Let's start building one together.

Here's where another mental shift is in order.

MENTAL SHIFT

If you connect vulnerably, intimately, and authentically to an audience, they'll forgive you nearly any kind of natural mistake or mishap. Being flawed and human are strengths, not weaknesses.

It is our unrealistic, often perfectionistic drives that make us think we must be flawless in front of an audience. If handled with humor and heart, our mistakes may not only be unimportant, they can serve to connect us more intimately with our listeners by showing our humanity and compassion.

Think about it: If you're an audience member and a speaker loses her train of thought, spills coffee, or stumbles in any way, do you dismiss what she's saying? Do you lose admiration for her? Of course not, not if she's built a connection to you and she laughs it off and moves on without letting it bother her.

Beware—the opposite of this mental shift is equally true. If you come across as cold, arrogant, indifferent, or ill-prepared, an audience will likely not feel connected, and small errors will become huge barriers. Authentic connection to listeners, to say nothing of a sense of humor, buys you huge leeway and eliminates the need for perfection. Knowing this is your safety net.

The "Too" Problem

"Cherish forever what makes you unique 'cuz you're really a yawn if it goes."
—Bette Midler, actor, singer

I hear a lot of people voice their fear by using the word *too*. *I'm too old. I'm too inexperienced. I'm too shy. I'm too young. I'm too unknown. I'm too overweight.*

If you are legitimately under-qualified to talk about a given topic, either get qualified or don't talk about it. Seems simple. That's not what the "too" problem is. What we're talking about here is unfounded self-doubt or what a lot of people call the "inner critic." This fear is uttered by some of the most highly qualified people in their fields.

I once coached a double-PhD chemist who had served as lead in discovering and developing a revolutionary pharmaceutical product. His amazing product will make the lives of lots of very sick people a whole lot easier. (I wish I could tell you all about it, but ethics require my confidentiality.) I coached him for an upcoming presentation of his team's research findings, a prototype, and business analysis to a group of venture capitalists in order to gain multimillion-dollar funding to bring the product to market. Despite his education, his qualifications—and what I assert is his freaking *genius*—this scientist feared that he was "too young" to be perceived as credible. He suggested that a more senior member of his team should make the pitch. "They'll never take me seriously and grant millions of dollars to someone they think of as a kid," he said. When I probed, I determined that though he had a youthful appearance, he was no more than a few years younger than the investors to whom he was presenting and senior by far to all of them in his experience and education. His perceived "too young" problem became a little laughable when we did the math. (He was the youngest of four brothers, so perhaps that was the root of his "too" problem.) Finally, he surrendered. "I think I'm just looking for something to disqualify myself, aren't I?"

When we feel we are "too" something, it's usually self-doubt and little more.

After crafting his story and practicing its delivery, my chemist client not only got his funding, he got more than triple what he requested. The investors saw not only the value of his idea, but also the importance of him being the public face of the product as it goes to market. His age was never a factor to them, just a smoke screen of his self-doubt and fear.

Imagine how powerful you'll be if you stop disqualifying yourself when there's no legitimate basis to do so. This is the work of your own inaccurate "inner critic," a voice worth learning to identify and ignore.

"I've been on a diet for two weeks and all I've lost is two weeks."
—Totie Fields, actress, comedian

I once coached a writer, helping her finish a novel. Her writing was skilled, her story a moving one. After much collaboration, her book neared the point where she could submit it to agents and publishers—her originally stated goal. "I can't submit it yet," she said. "I have to lose forty pounds first so that I'll look better on my jacket photo and if I go on a book tour." No amount of discussion, logic, or reassurance mattered.

How many writers—most of them women, I presume—have squelched their own opportunities because of shame and body image issues? To date, that writer never has submitted that work or any other for publication. Her "too" problem was *too* much for her to overcome.

The "too problem" often arises from either our family history or personal experience of someone asking that oh-so-damaging question in one of its hundreds of forms: *Who do you think you are?* This question is a scold for an act of confidence or boldness. It says, *You're nothing special. Go back to being small.* It says that you're "too" something. *Who do you think you are?* is rhetorical, and not meant for a rational reply. What should our voiced reply to it be? How about, *I'll tell you who I am. I'm me. Experience, knowledge, strengths, warts and all, with my utterly unique vantage on the world that's valuable enough to share. I'm me.*

Time to outgrow those old messages.

For many years I've written the following quote into the front of my datebook where I'll see it every day:

> **"Anything or anyone who does not bring you alive is too small for you."**
> —David Whyte, poet, philosopher

This "too" problem doesn't bring us more alive. Time to chuck it. Take *that*, inner critic!

The "Not Enough" Problem

> **"Comparison is the death of joy."**
> —Mark Twain

The fraternal twin of the "too" problem is the "not enough" problem. *I'm not smart enough. I'm not experienced enough. I'm not charismatic enough. I'm not funny enough. I'm not fill-in-the-blank enough.*

The "not enough" problem stems from comparison. We measure ourselves—and all of our perceived shortcomings—against someone we estimate as superior. Introverts envy extroverted presenters who appear at ease, funny, dynamic, engaging, and charismatic and think, "I could never be as good as *that*." Extroverts, who have plenty of dynamic energy, may envy a calm, poised, focused, self-possessed speaker, and say, "I could never be as good as *that*!" Others are more beautiful, more famous, more educated, more whatever. In the game of comparison, the one comparing always comes up short.

We compare our own speaking abilities to those of iconic orators in history, movie stars delivering memorized scripts written by Oscar-winning screenwriters, and even to TED Talk speakers who have prepared and practiced and often memorized their ten-to-eighteen-minute talks for *months*.

I cry foul! While I offer TED Talks as examples in this book so you can see what I'm writing about more vividly, I do not offer them as a way to compare our more informal talks to those that are rehearsed, often down to the word.

The irony here is that when they are in casual conversations, the same people who feel they are not funny/engaging/interesting/smart/calm/poised enough are often all of those things. In my casual encounters, the preponderance of my coaching clients are authentic, at ease, funny, engaging, confident, and so on. It's just when they stand up and feel that they're doing a "presentation"—when they're "public speaking"—that they clam up, look down, shut down, and indeed appear "not enough" for the task when they are more than qualified to speak about their topic.

Every suggestion I make in this book is to help you to bring your natural, most comfortable self to the front of your speaking opportunities. You. You're enough.

What If They Don't Like Me?

"There are very few monsters who warrant the fear we have of them."
—Andre Gide, author, Nobel prize winner

Most people never say aloud, *What if people don't like me?* Instead, it's often the unspoken undercurrent of what people fear. It's disguised as *What if I'm boring? What if they don't take me seriously?* There's nothing wrong with wanting to be liked. It's human nature.

Ironically, it is sometimes our fear of not being liked that causes us to stiffen up and flatten out. Our nerves can make us appear distant, angry, judgmental, or arrogant. *Our anxiety about not being likable can make us seem less likeable.* I know that seems a little like an M. C. Escher drawing folding back on itself, so let it sink in. Simply stated, our fears become reality . . . if we let them.

"Be yourself. Everyone else is already taken."
—Oscar Wilde

Here's the bad news: not everyone is going to like your books or your ideas.

I've attended many book clubs that selected one of my books for their group and invited me to attend, some in person and some via Skype or other video-conferencing platforms. These can be big fun. It's been my pleasure to enjoyed warm and wonderful evenings in a host's home, talking books with a group of book lovers.

In one book club, one of the readers of my novel was very tight-lipped as the rest chatted about the story and asked me loads of questions. Observing this, I invited all to participate in the discussion, and also reassured them that I'd truly welcome their honest reactions to the book—I had a feeling. The quiet one eventually spoke up, saying (as kindly as possible), "I'm so sorry, but I just didn't enjoy the book. It made me feel uncomfortable." I asked if she'd be willing to share why, because it might help me to learn something about my writing. "Because of all of the graphic sex," she finally confessed. She was not a fan of the intimate scenes between my two lead characters, nor of the potty-mouthed supporting character that the rest of the book club members said was their favorite. This reader held specific religious feelings and had legitimate personal objections to several of the story lines and themes in the book. To my sensibilities, the intimate scenes are tender, modest, and far from explicit, but that doesn't matter; to this reader, they were graphic.

I'll admit that this exchange was a little awkward at first. By resisting getting defensive, and by letting her know I respected her views, she was able to talk about the parts of the book she did enjoy. The whole group ended up laughing a lot, shared some wine, and talked about books, family, and travel. It turned out to be a lovely evening. That particular book club member doesn't like my book; I can live with that. If you're going to publish your books, whatever the genre, you'll meet some people who don't like them. If your book contains highly controversial topics, you may have a large percentage that don't like it. Not all of them will be as pleasant as my book club friend.

Here's a mini exercise for you. Select a popular book that you love. Go onto Amazon or Goodreads, look that book up, and read the reviews. You'll see lots of praise. You'll likely also find some pretty harsh criticism. I loved Cheryl Strayed's memoir *Wild,* a highly popular *New York Times* bestseller. It boasts hundreds of glowing online reviews. It also has some scathing ones and a few that are downright nasty. Some people didn't like it because it wasn't really about hiking. One reviewer called it "self-pitying navel gazing." Many had objections to language, to sexual choices, and to what they perceived to be animal mistreatment in the story.

Reading the reviews of *Wild* made me feel pretty good about my having the occasional reader, reviewer, or audience member who doesn't love my book. I'm in good company. The art to handling criticism is to not take it personally and to respond with grace.

I Don't Like When Everybody Is Looking at Me

"I'd rather be looked over than overlooked."
—Mae West

While we crave attention for our books, many writers feel ambivalent, or even terrified, of having all eyes on us.

What we might not realize is that our discomfort with being "seen" could be robbing us of opportunities for doing things that offer great meaning, pleasure, or satisfaction. I still prefer dinner with a few friends to a big party, but today, this fear of being seen does not keep me from welcoming opportunities to do what matters to me, and occasionally that means being the center of attention for a few moments at a time. The question arises from Mae West's quote: Would *you* rather be looked over than be overlooked? If you're willing to be overlooked you're saying that you want your book to be overlooked as well.

Allowing our momentary discomfort at being "seen" to rob us of the experience of sharing our writing and our ideas with others is a huge waste. Plus, gaining the skills we'll cover in parts 2 and 3 can reduce the discomfort by a great deal.

Some of our fear of being "looked at" has to do with that self-consciousness about our bodies or our appearance. It can come from a feeling of having our stories—percolated in our heart and minds, written while we're alone—so conspicuously out in the world. It's a vulnerable feeling. Let me offer a shift in thinking about this one:

MENTAL SHIFT

Vulnerability in both writing and in speaking can be your biggest asset.
Though it may feel uncomfortable to have your ideas and emotions on display, it is often the most vulnerable speakers who inspire us most deeply. If you can embrace and welcome the feeling of vulnerability rather than protecting yourself from it, you'll be the stronger artist and the stronger speaker for it. Audiences will reward you by their response.

Here's the good news—the really good news: The rewards for being our true selves as we speak in public can, and often do, overshadow the fear of feeling exposed as we get more experience. The following two quotes from the same author illustrate this nicely:

"Courage starts with showing up and letting ourselves be seen."
"The willingness to show up changes us. It makes us a little braver each time."
—Brené Brown, from *Daring Greatly: How the Courage To Be Vulnerable Transforms the Way We Live, Love, Parent, and Lead*

I've both witnessed and experienced the transition that these two quotes describe. Showing up and letting ourselves be our most honest, vulnerable selves ultimately results in courage. If we wait for courage to arrive, it never does. If we act courageously, and show up, courage arrives. In the same way, we must sometimes write before our muse arrives, and long before we're confident in what we're writing. It's when you start writing that the moody muse decides to show up. Courage is like that, too.

What If I Cry? Freeze? Trip? Or Goof Up Big Time?

"The quickest way to acquire self-confidence is to do exactly what you are afraid to do."
—Anonymous

Now we're getting specific.

My clients, across all kinds of industries, have shared anxiety about their autonomic responses (tears, freezing up, panicking, getting hives, shaking, sweating, digestive trouble, the list goes on) that they avoid public speaking for fear that one or more might happen. It's important to know that it is not the *reality* of public speaking that causes sweaty palms, hives, trembling, or digestive problems; it is the *fear* of it that causes these maladies.

Forgetting what you're going to say or losing your train of thought is a common experience for most speakers, newbies and those with boatloads of experience. It happens *all the time* and to everyone. Do what the experienced speakers do: *Roll with it. Relax. It'll come to you.* People won't judge you harshly if you lose your train of thought, but they'll judge you harshly if you freak out about losing your thought, especially if you let it taint the rest of your talk.

The fear of forgetting is often key to the rest of these symptoms. Good preparation for your talk and having simple notes as backup will prevent most public memory loss along with quelling some of the anxiety. We'll get to that in part 2. The real trick for this worry is to relax and trust that you know your topic and can retrieve the ideas you need to.

Here's a way to think about it. You're in the grocery store. You've gone through the whole store thinking you got everything on your mental list. Then, you're standing in the checkout line and it comes to you—*Sour cream! I forgot sour cream!* Why did the idea come to you right then?

The answer is simple: because you were standing still, doing nothing. You knew you needed sour cream. The knowledge was in you. You simply forgot in the distraction of your shopping. It came to you when you paused for a moment. The same is true for speaking.

TIP: If you lose your train of thought, simply stand still, pause, put a pleasant, neutral expression on your face (like you've planned this all along) and breathe. Take a sip of water. Check your notes if you need to. The thought will come back to you. If it doesn't, move on. Nobody will be the wiser.

Let's face it—if you give lots of presentations, some will be better than others and occasionally you'll have an off day. Preparing and learning the skills I'll cover in this book will increase your average by a big bunch, but everybody has days when they're "in the zone", or when they're a bit off. I've delivered thousands of hours of training, coaching, and speaking. Not every moment would get an A in my own mind—the burden of having high standards—even when the participants gave me high marks. Accepting this disparity as well as the fact that even when I give a stellar class, the occasional participant may not like it, my message, or me, has freed me of worrying about it. I'm not going to say I love it when a class isn't up to my standards, just that it's occasionally true. The more you speak, the better you'll get, but perfection and one hundred percent approval cannot be the goal.

I've gotten the hiccups during a recorded teleseminar I was delivering. While I'm usually quick at learning and remembering names, I've suffered the occasional memory block that caused me to call a participant by the wrong name—multiple times. *Ugh*. I accidentally cursed when I spilled coffee during a talk for a conservative religious non-profit group. I had to enact several unscheduled, and sudden breaks during a day-long talk because of, *ahem*, biological imperatives. If you speak a lot, mishaps, misspeaking, and flat out mistakes will occasionally occur. But I'm here to tell the tale. I didn't die. I didn't get fired. I'm invited back.

Most audience members will accept human errors and mishaps. It's all about how you handle them. Do they unravel you, or do you roll with them? Do you have a sense of humor about it, or does your inner perfectionist come out and cause you to show your frustration? When you get to the end of part 1, I invite you to watch Lizzie Velasquez's TEDx Talk listed in the Make It Stick section to follow. There are tons of reasons to be inspired by it. I invite you to focus on what she does when she loses her train of thought . . . right in the middle of her highly prepared, über-practiced TED Talk. Everyone's nightmare, right? Notice how she handles her own brief memory lapse. Notice how the audience responds. Spoiler . . . she does great!

CHAPTER 2

Why Leave Your Studio? Rewards for
Writers Who Speak

*"Not everything that can be counted counts,
and not everything that counts can be counted."*
—Albert Einstein, theoretical physicist

I once held a romantic Emily Dickinson-esque image of the writer's life in my mind. I envisioned myself sitting alone in my book-filled studio, daydreaming and writing stories that magically found their way into the world. Readers would write me letters on scented paper, in calligraphic hand, and I'd invite them to come to my parlor for tea—one, or perhaps a small few at a time. I imagined someone else—an agent or a publishing sales rep—placing my book in stores all over the country. I had only to stay in my studio or my garden and write more stories, emerging occasionally to share tea with insightful readers.

It was a lovely little fantasy.

If we want our writing to be experienced by more than just our small collection of acquaintances, we have to find ways for it to first get out of our heads and onto the page, then for it to get out into the world. Lots of writers—as well as other artists and creative people—are more comfortable creating their art than they are with the "business" of gaining visibility for that art: publicity, marketing, and speaking.

"I used to say 'no' much more often than I do now. This is a nicer way to live."
—Holly Hunter, actor

If I'm going to leave my Dickinson-esque parlor and stand in front of others, I need to know the reasons for doing so, and they'd better be good. Some rewards are quantifiable; others are less so, but important nonetheless. Getting comfortable with the public part of your private writing life is a transition that requires some motivation. For me, the rewards to writers for public speaking fall into six basic categories. These are just some of the payoffs for exiting your parlor, learning the skills, and speaking about your writing and your ideas to listeners and audience. Let's look at them in detail.

REWARD #1: TO SELL BOOKS

> *"Publishers want authors who are regularly in front of crowds of people. Why? Because this sells books."*
> —Brooke Warner, from *What's Your Book?: A Step-by-Step Guide to Get You from Inspiration to Published Author*

While all of us want our books to sell, some of us have to come to terms with the idea of *selling* books. Some creative people get squirmy when they think of marketing their art. I get it.

As a shy kid—a *really* shy kid—I got kicked out of (or strongly encouraged to leave) my Girl Scout troop by my den mother because I declined to sell cookies. The idea of talking to neighbors and strangers was so loathsome and intimidating that I couldn't bring myself to do it for any amount of merit badges. My scout leader was rabidly competitive with a neighboring troop. As one unable or unwilling to sell cookies, I was not an asset to her ambition to be the top-selling troop in the region. She said I'd be "dead weight" on the group if I didn't sell my share. (I know! As a mother, I'd like to go back in time and, *ahem*, enlighten her, but that's another book.)

It's often early, negative messages that fuel our adult fears and cause us to form inaccurate assumptions and attitudes that we hold for years. I had it in my head from early on that I was *not* a salesperson. In adulthood, I decided I never wanted to have a job selling anything.

Selling—only in my limited thinking—seemed tacky, pushy, and not me. To be sales-y was to be a huckster, a snake-oil salesman. Let's face facts: if we have any ambition for making money as writers, or even just getting the ideas of our book out into the world, selling is an inevitable part of the process. While we may write for reasons of our own healing, creativity, or personal expression, there's also a commerce aspect to the writing life. If you want to make money as a writer, you have to sell books. Time for a mental shift!

Writers' appearances are what make one author's books stand out from the crowd of hundreds of thousands of new books that come out every year. I can't tell you how many books I've bought because I heard the author on National Public Radio or saw him on a talk show, or went to see her when she spoke at my local bookstore. I bet you have, too. Don't *sell* it to me; make me *want* it.

I'll never be a sales person in the way my misguided den mother wanted me to be, selling a product I don't care about just to hit some set of numbers. I'm proud of my books and I'm not ashamed to talk about them with passion and enthusiasm. If you're not, who will be?

REWARD #2: TO BUILD A COMMUNITY

"Generosity is the new currency."
—Kamy Wicoff, author, founder of SheWrites.com and cofounder of She Writes Press

Having a community is an important element of a writer's life before, during, and after publication. By doing live readings of both published and yet-to-be-published stories and poetry, taking part in (and possibly hosting) literary events, and connecting to other writers at conferences, in classes, and in literary organizations, you can begin to build your writing community long before you're published, and it'll be right there waiting for you when you do. These will be your champions, your encouragers, and your pool of resources. These are your peers.

If you're anything like me, some will become dear friends.

"Being a writer is like having an illness, and the pain is alleviated by scratching on a piece of paper."
—Suzan-Lori Parks, playwright

The beauty of being part of a writing community is that we all share the same "illness," as Suzan-Lori Parks describes it. We understand one another. We understand—and hopefully celebrate—one another's milestones and accomplishments. Connecting to other writers and publishing professionals in both online and in-person communities can be a source of encouragement for your writing and for your speaking endeavors. These are the people who understand our neuroses, sympathize with our doubts, and help us to identify when the voice of our inner critic is halting us.

Readers can also become a vital part of your community. Making an authentic, personal connection at live events can turn audience members into readers, readers into fans, and fans into super fans. Super fans not only buy a book, they give it as gifts, choose it for book clubs, promote it on social networks, and tell friends about what they've read and how delightful the author was in person. Some write glowing reviews for our books. Invaluable.

Community goes both ways. It's important to be a supporter of other writers by attending their writing events when you can. Attend readings, book launches, poetry slams, and open-mike events. Tell the bookstore events manager how glad you are that she brought that author to the shop, preferably with a couple of purchased books under your arm. Be the kind of supporter to other writers that you'd like for yourself. Well-attended events that promote sales give booksellers the incentive to host more such events—perhaps even your own. When we spend the "currency" of generosity to other writers as well as to booksellers, the dividends are incalculable.

As a bonus benefit, by attending author events, you get to observe other writers as presenters. You can see which events (and which speakers) inspire you to buy their books. You can observe which authors connect to you and which put you off, and more importantly, why they put you off. You can see the range of speaking skills—some dynamic and others less so. Observe the skills of other authors in order to learn from them. You can observe which book launches are fun and lively, or moving and inspiring, and which fall flat. I think of this as free speakers' school. Take notes. Gather ideas that you'd like to use at your own events.

REWARD #3: TO CONNECT OUR WRITING TO A CAUSE

Our writing reflects who we are and what we value. Sometimes a cause emerges as an integral part of, or an adjunct to, the written story. Other times, it's just a value that the writer holds and she uses her platform as an author to bring light to a personal, cultural, or political passion that is apart from your book's topic. Now and then, you may want to use a book event as a fundraiser for a cause that you value, but is unrelated to your book. A few examples:

- My friend and long-time writing partner Amy S. Peele wrote *Cut: A Medical Murder Mystery.* Amy describes her book as "a mystery with a mission." It's a delightful romp designed for pure entertainment. What makes this mystery special is that Amy brought to her story her expertise and experience as a nurse and administrator in the organ transplant field in some of the most prestigious and cutting-edge medical facilities in the US. *Cut*, in addition to being a fun mystery, lets readers into the fascinating, often-unseen world of organ donation and transplantation. At the end of her book, Amy offers readers information about how to register to be organ donors. At each of her talks, she mentions the importance of donation, and encourages audiences to talk to their loved ones about their wishes so that they have clarity if they're ever faced with a family tragedy. Amy isn't pushy or preachy. She uses humor and heart, drawing people to her cause rather than pushing them. Whatever her royalty statement says, Amy reports that her biggest reward to date has been the people who've told her that they signed up as organ donors after reading her book.

- Sometimes a cause is not a specific action that an author wants a reader to take, but an attitude that an author wants to influence or new light she wants to shed on a topic. Sue Monk Kidd, author of *The Secret Life of Bees,* is an author icon of mine and I went to see her when she was touring to launch *The Invention of Wings.* Kidd is a historical fiction writer whose books often feature themes about the interactions between black and white people throughout the history of the American South. In addition to her candor, intelligence, and elegance, I came away struck by what Kidd said about why she writes books about this topic. She said that as a white Southern woman she felt an "onus of responsibility" to research, understand, and write about the history of how black people have been and are being treated in American culture. She said, without a hint of arrogance, that she wanted to use her "gift" to do good. Hers is a different kind of mission. She's not raising money. She's not asking people to act. She only wants to shed light upon the wrong of our shared history by telling the truth about it—through fiction. Lucky for us, she does this with extraordinary literary gifts.

- Whatever your topic, whatever your genre, my guess is that there is an issue, topic, or perspective important to you that emerges in your writing. David Sedaris (memoir) wants to entertain and make people laugh at absurdity. Pam Houston's writing (fiction and memoir) always perpetuates an appreciation of animals and nature. Brené Brown (nonfiction) wants us to heal from shame. Your cause might be more playful—say, getting people to take up snowboarding, teaching someone to laugh at herself, or inspiring an appreciation for folk art. It may be to change an attitude or inspire curiosity. Or it may be more action-oriented, like encouraging eco-activism or preventing gun violence.

  Speaking, and doing it well, can bring opportunities to shed light on the issues and attitudes that matter to you most.

REWARD #4: SPEAKING BEGETS SPEAKING AND OTHER COOL OPPORTUNITIES

Most authors do not make their entire living from the books they write, even well established authors. I know—*bummer*. If you are an engaging speaker, you reveal your skills to a wider world, creating potential for other opportunities and income.

Years before I published my memoir, *Filling Her Shoes*, I read one of the stories that was later included in it at a small-town reading series. In the audience, unbeknownst to me, was a woman whose cousin was looking for a ghostwriter who could write with "heart." She liked my story and passed my name to her cousin, who called me, and I ended up with a paid ghostwriting opportunity that I'd never even imagined, much less sought out. I was simply reading a memoir piece in polished draft form that I wasn't then sure I'd ever publish. That reading resulted in a paid writing gig right in the middle of The Great Recession.

Some authors teach workshops or act as consultants, either in their field of expertise or on the techniques and process of writing. Sometimes the books they publish are simply a means to an end, to establish themselves as experts in a given field.

Speaking begets speaking . . . and a lot of other unanticipated opportunities.

REWARD #5: TO HAVE THE WRITER'S 3-D EXPERIENCE— WITHOUT THE FUNNY GLASSES

> **"'Tis the good reader that makes the good book."**
> **—Ralph Waldo Emerson**

The 3-D experience is a cool reward and one every writer should have the opportunity to experience.

Our stories are only partly complete when we write them. It is what the reader brings to and takes from the story that catapults it from the flat surface of the page and makes it three-dimensional.

I urge every writer to start reading his work in public, even before publication—at poetry slams, at reading salons, on panels, to critique groups. It was the responses of the listeners to early drafts of my work that let me know when I was on to something with a story, and when my emotional intention in writing it was met (or not). I could hear which sections fell flat or moved too slowly. When listeners laughed at the funny parts, audibly "oohed" or gasped at the shocking parts, or teared up during poignant scenes, I was surprised by the thrill of it. My story *mattered* to someone, touched someone. I'd never have known this if I hadn't summoned my courage and read stories in public. It was these experiences that changed me from being a lifelong writer to an aspiring author.

"The words rise to glory when we give them away."
—Dorothy Allison, author

When I heard Dorothy Allison utter the words above at a live event she shared with Karen Joy Fowler, something in my bones hummed. I wrote them down and have thought about them often in the years since.

Though writing is so much a solitary act—and for that I treasure it—once written, our stories become interactive in the hearts and minds of other humans. When someone says that your story made him laugh, got her through a dark time, let her know she is not alone, or inspired him to view his circumstances in a new light, that's a good day—a *very* good day for a writer.

I didn't start out writing thinking that the reader's involvement was important, but I have come to know that it is, indeed, one of the reasons I write, and the main reason that I publish what I write. Don't we want to touch, move, inspire, humor, entertain, enlighten, horrify, shock, disrupt, and otherwise affect our readers? Reading and speaking in public lets us experience this most directly, most immediately, and most intimately. I urge you not to let fear or nerves make you miss out on this experience. It is among the sweetest of rewards.

REWARD #6: BECAUSE, DAMMIT, FEAR SHOULDN'T WIN!

"Hello, fear. Thank you for being here. You're my indication that I'm doing what I needed to do."
—Cheryl Strayed, author of *Wild* and *Brave Enough*

I'll confess a guilty pleasure: I love the TV show *The Voice*, and not primarily for the music. The celebrity coaches serve as mentors and champions for every singer on the show, even those not on their teams. Their messages and coaching are often as fitting for me, as a writer, as they are to the singing contestants. Pharrell Williams served as a mentor one season and was helping a young contestant overcome her profound stage fright. She had battled nerves her whole life, even to the point of having panic attacks that made her give up performing for several years. Here she was facing performing on national stage. Imagine! Her coach stopped rehearsal and said to her:

"If you've been afraid and it's never resulted in any kind of positivity, why would you invite fear to this moment?"
—Pharrell Williams, musician, songwriter, music producer

I paused my TV to write that one down. (I always have a notebook with me: during movies, book events, and even in the car. Pulling my car over to take note of an inspiring message or brilliant quote is a common occurrence for me.) I'd never thought about the fact that I was *inviting* fear to the special moments of my own life. I strive to consciously *disinvite* it now. Wisdom and inspiration are available everywhere, even a TV contest show.

Fear does not deserve to win or to stop you. It doesn't even deserve an invitation to your party! Frankly, it makes me angry to think that I once let fear rule me and cause me to miss out on experiences that matter to me. It breaks my heart when I see someone else letting fear win.

Please, dear writers, artists, musicians, activists, and creative entrepreneurs, don't let fear keep you from pursuing your passion. It's such a waste of who you are.

> **"Step out of the history that is holding you back. Step into the story you are willing to create."**
> —Oprah Winfrey, talk show host, actor, producer

Another Confession

Here, at the end of this chapter, I'll make another small confession. To this day my inner glossophobe still lives. She (that terrified one) has a smaller voice than she once did and only gets my ear when she's in cahoots with my inner critic. I get nervous before every talk—sometimes just a little, sometimes more. When the stakes are especially high, the subject is new, or the audience is unfamiliar, I have moments of trepidation and doubt.

What has quelled those nerves most is knowing that nerves are not always evidence of fear. They are also evidence of investment and excitement. When we care about something, when it matters to us, it's reasonable that our hearts may flutter faster. I now reframe my "nerves" before a speaking event. Rather than calling the feeling "nervousness" or "fear," I rename it excitement and anticipation. I invite you to give it a try.

In part 1, We have focused on the "why" of public speaking for writers. We've explored fear factors as well as the reasons and rewards that are available for writers who choose to develop their speaking skills.

I invite you to take inventory of any negative assumptions you might be holding. Make yourself open to the idea that, whatever skill level you possess, there is value in developing your speaking voice, just as there is in developing your writer's voice. Not only that, but it's doable for anyone who is motivated.

In part 2, we'll focus on the "what" of public speaking: what to say and how to select, deselect, and organize prepared content for any talk.

Before you move on to part 2, I invite you to do the following exercises and follow the links for deeper learning.

Make It Stick

EXERCISE #1: REFLECTION
Reflect on the following and make notes:

1. What experiences have you had in the past that "taught" you to be afraid of speaking in public? What happened? What was said? Who said it? Was it true? Is it still true?
2. What gains do you hope to achieve that could be enhanced by learning to speak with power, authority, and confidence?
3. What 3-D experiences have you had listening to or seeing authors speak in public?
4. What opportunities can you imagine might be opened up for you if you gain confidence and skill at speaking and reading your work in public?
5. What causes, ideas, or information have you been inspired to explore because you heard an author speak about her book?
6. What causes or ideas (from fun hobbies to vital issues) might you bring attention to if you speak about them? What impact might you have? What would this mean to you?

EXERCISE #2: TEDX TALK, BROOKE WARNER, GREEN-LIGHT REVOLUTION

After watching Brooke Warner's TEDx Talk, make notes about the following:

1. What nuggets did you gain from her message? What cause does she speak about?
2. What did you notice about the content and the delivery of her presentation?
3. How might you be "red-lighting" your writing life and perhaps your potential endeavors as a speaker?
4. What steps might you need to take to "green-light" your writing life and your opportunities to speak in public?

EXERCISE #3: TED TALK, LIZZIE VELASQUEZ, "HOW DO YOU DEFINE YOURSELF?"

After watching, make notes about the following:

1. What parts of Lizzie's talk can you apply to yourself?
2. Notice how she handles it when she loses her train of thought. Did your opinion of her sustain damage because of this error? If so, why? If not, why not?
3. What role did humor play in this talk?

 EXERCISE #4: *MAKING YOUR MIND MAGNIFICENT* BY STEVEN CAMPBELL

This material is available in both book and audio form. While either is useful, I enjoyed the audio version a lot. It's great for driving time. Campbell has spent years studying how we can tap into the resources of our brain to actually change the way we operate personally and professionally in the world. It's inspiring, encouraging, and informative. You can see/hear samples of his soft-spoken but inspiring talks, as well as links to his book and audio, by going to his website.

EXERCISE #5: *ON WORD,* AN AUTHORS' VLOG

Find these super-short videos of renown authors, talking craft, inspiration, process, and more. Find them at OnWordTalks.com

These are clearly experienced authors and their talks are edited. After enjoying a few (I just love them) make note of what speaking qualities you observe. Which author talks appeal to you? Which ones intrigue you about reading their books? What do you notice about style, authenticity, and humor?

Enjoy!

PART 2

What To Say

"You're the only one in the room who can tell the story as only you would."
—Lidia Yuknavitch, author

In part 1 we addressed the "inside work," the fear factors and misconceptions about public speaking and the value to writers for speaking with authenticity and confidence: the "why" of public speaking.

In part 2, we'll address the "outside work," the "what" of public speaking: designing the content for any talk. I'll be specific and detailed, offering tools and methods for preparing and delivering what you're going to say at your book events, or for any presentation you want to make. The tools are here to help you select, deselect, and organize your spoken content.

We will cover:

- Determining your goal for every talk
- Charting the course of your talk with all of the elements of a *Story Map*
- Adding *Spellbinders* to entrance listeners
- Where to add "thank-yous"
- Practicing and revising talks and creating usable speaker notes

CHAPTER 3

Determine Your Intention for Every Talk

"After nourishment, shelter, and companionship, stories are the thing we need most in the world."
—Philip Pullman, author of the *His Dark Materials* series

Step close. Let me whisper this important mental shift in your ear. *As a writer, you already possess the most difficult-to-learn and important skill for powerful public speaking.* When it comes to preparing the content of a spoken presentation, writers start leagues ahead of most speakers. We are storytellers.

Writing and speaking are different in some ways, alike in others. At their best, both are storytelling. You, writer friend, come to speaking with an appreciation for and facility with the most dynamic elements of storytelling—language, metaphor, suspense, pace, emotional contrast, understanding of conflict, and much more—where other speakers often find these to be challenging.

With storytelling skills in your pocket, what most writers need is some structure and a simple and efficient way to select, deselect, and organize their thoughts into the most vivid story they can tell about their books or their topics.

I call the model I'm offering here a *Story Map*.

Just as in writing, when we speak we are asking others to join us on a journey that we've designed—a story journey. When going through new territory, it's awfully nice to have a guide who knows the route and can keep the trip on course.

"If you fail to plan, you plan to fail."
—Benjamin Franklin, American founding father

Are You a Prepper or a Pantser?

Martha Alderson, author of *The Plot Whisperer: Secrets of Story Structure Any Writer Can Master,* and *Writing Blockbuster Plots: A Step-by-Step Guide to Mastering Plot, Structure, and Scene,* sorts writers into two categories: plotters and pantsers. By this she means that some writers—plotters—design and plan their plots before they begin writing a book or a story. Some do this in elaborate detail. Others write with a vague idea of their story, but prefer to make their plot up as they go along—by the seats of their pants. Alderson offers a deceptively simple, and highly useful tool called the *Plot Planner* that can help both styles of writers. She is agnostic about the styles of plotters and pantsers, stating that each has its advantages and disadvantages in the writing process.

The same is true for speakers. There are those who want to prepare and either memorize or read every word they're going to say, like a script. I call these speakers "preppers", (akin to Alderson's "plotters"). Others want to prepare little or not at all, preferring to wing it in front of the group and hope for the best. I've used Alderson's "pantsers" term for these speakers.

Often, more introverted speakers are preppers, nervous that they'll lose their nerve (and their memories) in front of a group. Scripted—whether read or memorized—content in a less formal setting can be comforting to these preppers, but they risk coming across as aloof and distant, rather than connected and vibrant. Extroverts tend to be more comfortable with working on the fly, which can make their talks lively and spontaneous. But they risk coming across as disorganized, less credible, and running out of time without accomplishing what they'd hoped.

I'm with Martha Alderson on this; each of these styles—prepper and pantser—has its pluses and minuses. The tools that I'll cover in this section offer a hybridized solution suited both for those who like to feel prepared, and those who prefer spontaneity.

Let me make an important distinction here. A scripted "speech," prepared and memorized, or read (sometimes from a teleprompter), is a comparatively rare kind of talk for most writers. Such formal "speeches" are more common for political events, valedictorian addresses, TED Talks, and some keynote addresses and not our more frequent kinds of talks. While the Story Map is an ideal tool for organizing content for scripted talks as well as more casual ones, writers more commonly use it as a map rather than a verbatim script.

Don't Let Words Get In the Way

"A writer is someone for whom writing is more difficult than it is for other people."
—Thomas Mann, author

Writers by nature are word lovers. I often find, ironically, that it is writers who get most paralyzed about what words they're going to use as they prepare for public presentations. We get tangled in the weeds over the details of our sentences and spend inordinate amounts of time wordsmithing rather than designing a memorable talk that's tailored to our goals and our listeners. By focusing on the words first and not the message, we risk ending up with a disjointed talk with pretty words, but without a compelling message or "story".

I ask you here to be open to a different way of preparing the content of a talk than you might have used in the past or learned in school. It might feel peculiar at first, but what doesn't when it's new? Once it's worn in and familiar, my clients and students end up loving this method and use it for not only the specific event they've hired me to help them prepare for, but for all subsequent presentations.

Here's my prediction: Use the Story Map as I describe it five times and I predict you'll use it, or some elements of it, for every single talk you deliver.

Packing for Your Trip: What Do You Want from Your Journey?

A story is an invitation to take readers or listeners on a journey. The storyteller is the designated tour guide, designing and delivering that story. (By "storyteller," I mean speaker. This does not imply that what the storyteller is saying isn't true, only that truthful and important information of all kinds can and should be delivered in a storytelling style to engage listeners.)

Before we depart for a planned travel journey of nearly any kind, there are four basic questions that we need to answer:

1. **Goal:** Where do I want to go?
2. **Companions:** Who's going with me, and what are their needs?
3. **Logistics:** How long will the journey be and how am I getting there?
4. **Style:** What kind of experience do I want to have for myself, and my traveling companions?

Answering these four questions clarifies a lot about how we need to plan for a shared trip. It doesn't make sense to book travel and start packing a bag until we've determined the destination, know whom our fellow travelers will be, and the length and logistics of the trip. The same is true for planning a talk.

To demonstrate the Story Map and how to prepare your content, I'll use a specific presentation scenario: a book launch. With her permission, I'm using a book launch preparation created with and by a specific author—in this case a debut novelist—whom I coached before her launch. This tool is equally applicable to any genre, any content, and indeed any style of talk you want to deliver.

The Story Map Preparation

Though we share the same publisher, Catherine Marshall-Smith and I hadn't met prior to my own memoir launch in May of 2017, which was just a few weeks before the scheduled launch of her debut novel, *American Family*. Catherine attended my launch, liked what she'd heard, and later asked if she could use my consultation services to prepare her own launch talk. (Remember the benefits of speaking I mentioned in part 1? I include my coaching for speakers work in my bio, which is read as part of my introduction by the host. No "selling"—just attracting.)

Let's set the scene. Catherine's pub date loomed. She'd booked a date at a local indie bookstore for the launch. She was nervous. Despite her decades of experience as a middle-school teacher, speaking publicly as an author about a deeply personal and potentially controversial topic was new to her. By looking at Catherine's preparation for her talk, you'll know better how to do your own.

Packing for Your Speaking Journey

Prior to crafting the specifics of your content, I urge you, as I did Catherine, to ask yourself four questions similar to the ones I posed in planning for a journey:

Question 1: What do I hope to accomplish with this talk? (*Your goal*)
Question 2: What is my best assessment of who will be in the audience and what matters to them? (*Assessment of "companions' needs" or, in the case of presentations, listeners*)
Question 3: How much time do I have to speak, and what is the setting like? (*Logistics*)
Question 4: What kind of experience do you want to have for yourself and your listeners during your talk? (*Style*)

Let's go through Catherine's pre-trip preparation step-by-step.

STEP 1: YOUR GOAL

To get at the answer to Catherine's first question—her goal—we had a conversation about how her book was born, what themes it contains, and if she had an idea, a cause, or a message that arises from her novel that she wanted to share.

American Family, published in spring of 2017, is a novel about a gay dad in conflict with his deceased ex-wife's conservative Christian parents over the custody of his ten-year-old daughter. It's a complex, nuanced story with characters both flawed and virtuous on both sides—the best kind of story.

Catherine's story originated from her personal crisis of faith. Being a person for whom her church has been a source of strength and comfort, and having many loved ones and close friends in the LGBT community, she struggled with how her faith was being defined by others, in conflict with her own beliefs. A faith that was once a source of soothing relief had become a barrier between Catherine and the loved ones she held dear. This was the seed of her story and the dilemma her characters face. The goal in her talk (as in her novel) was to tell this story without judgment, and to intrigue listeners of faith as well as those without a specific religion in the nuances of the topic. She didn't want to preach, but wanted to put compassionate light on all sides of this controversial issue.

STEP 2: WHO'S IN THE ROOM?

For her book launch, Catherine expected a diverse adult audience. Many would be friends, family members, and colleagues, but some could be unknown to her as either guests of others or walk-ins. There would be members of her church as well as gay friends. She was concerned about a strong reaction, even hot challenges, from audience members who had passionate points of view on both sides of the issue of conservative Christian faith and LGBT community concerns. She was launching her book in the context of a contentious year in United States politics; sensitivities were high.

STEP 3: LOGISTICS

The event would be at Book Passage, a renowned independent bookstore in Marin County, just north of San Francisco. The room is open and can accommodate sixty to one hundred people. Bookstore patrons can wander in during the event. The children's section is in an adjacent building. (An important factor if you're using strong language or reading adult material.)

There'd be a microphone, a raised podium, a lectern, and an attentive bookstore staff provided (not all bookstores can offer all of these luxuries). The store would handle sales, and the books had been ordered and had arrived. (Always worth checking a week or two before your event. Stuff happens.) Snacks and drinks, including alcohol, were welcomed, but not provided. The talking portion of the event was given no more than one hour, preferably about thirty-five minutes, plus question-and-answer (Q&A), but social time can linger.

STEP 4: STYLE

The tone of Catherine's talk was important to her. She wanted a fun, celebratory atmosphere, but she wanted more than that. She wanted her talk to be nonjudgmental, openhearted, loving, and inclusive of different kinds of thinking about her topic. She wanted to tell her truth, but had no axe to grind against anyone's belief system or political slant.

Answering these four questions is like pre-trip planning. It takes a bit of time, but the experience is much smoother as a result. The answers to these questions are not mere theory—they become the foundation of the talk you'll design. With these four questions thoughtfully considered, it's now time to create the Story Map.

In the following few chapters, we'll use the answers to these questions as foundational pieces for designing the content of a typical author talk.

CHAPTER 4

Chart the Course of Your Talk:
Using a Story Map

"If you don't know where you're going, you might end up someplace else."
—Yogi Berra, renown major league baseball coach

Completing the four questions that I posed to Catherine Marshall-Smith in chapter 3 was the first prep work for mapping her talk. If public speaking is a journey, many writers tend to start deciding what to put in their suitcase (the specific words) before they think about their destination. The risk here is that you can pack the wrong stuff. Who wants to lug winter boots if he's going to Tahiti?

Tools for Building Your Story Map

Once you've gone through the four questions in chapter 3, you're ready to start organizing your content—what you're going to say. Notice that I call this a Story Map. It's not a script, not an outline. It functions like a simple map that gives you markers to find your way through your prepared material. Designed well, it also becomes a single-page set of notes you can use during a talk.

For this, you'll need two pieces of "super high tech" equipment (not).

1. A piece of standard 8.5 x 11 paper or a printed Story Map (page 36). You can photocopy and enlarge the Story Map in this chapter to fit standard paper. A much more workable size.
2. Small Post-its, specifically the 1-⅜ x 1-⅞ size. Multiple colors are optional, but useful.

A Vote for Low Tech

The process I use for creating a Story Map is low tech by design. It's meant to tap into your freer thinking, your imaginative and creative, even playful self, not unlike writing freehand can be a way to let your ideas flow as you're starting to create a written story. Manipulating Post-its rather than typing our initial ideas gives us the psychological sensation that our ideas are flexible and editable. You can crumple the Post-its, rearrange them, and use alternately colored Post-its to draw your attention to important items you don't want to miss. (Oh, how I wish I were getting royalties from the 3M corporation for how much I've promoted Post-its in the last twenty years!)

Once we type words into a document—despite cut and paste options—there's a feeling that it's fixed. It makes our thinking rigid. The Story Map is your process piece in the planning stage.

"I am writing a first draft and reminding myself that I am simply shoveling sand into a box so that later I can build castles."
—Shannon Hale, author

Once you've got your Story Map just how you like it, it becomes your notes for practicing, and even delivering, your talk. (More details on that in chapter 10.)

By writing the elements of the Story Map—and, as part of it, the Introduction, or what I call the *Setup*—on Post-its and affixing them to the map in their designated spots, your content will feel flexible and editable.

In your initial planning of a road trip, what do you do? Pull out the map, right? Just to get the potential layout for the journey. For the sake of my metaphor, I'm going to pretend we're all in 1990 right now, pre-GPS technology; we're talking paper maps here. The Story Map is nothing like a thick atlas, crammed with optional routes and the names of every street you're not taking—it's more like a simple map you might draw so that you can glance at it while you're driving to make sure you're still on course. You look at the map before starting, but reference it now and then when you need to be reminded of landmarks and upcoming turns.

"Writing for the ear versus writing for the eye are two very different art forms."
—Sarah Hurwitz, speechwriter for Michelle Obama

How much information and detail go onto your written map? The answer is simple: just enough to get you to your destination without lengthy, unintentional detours. Too much information on your map and you'd have to pull over to read it. The same is true for your Story Map. You're building a developmental tool for your talk. Afterward, it becomes a simple map that helps you to practice and deliver your talk.

Get the Lay of the Land With A Story Map Overview

I invite you now to examine the entire Story Map on page •••. We'll refer back to it many times, and we'll break each element down in subsequent chapters.

Many corporations and communications training companies use various versions of a planning tool for spoken presentations. While each has their proprietary language—none used here—the earliest credit for identifying some of the elements of opening a talk should be attributed to Barbara Minto, author of *The Pyramid Principle*. Other tools emphasize sales or branding, use of in-house corporate language, or communicating business data. I've adapted the Story Map and its elements to work better for messages that writers and other creatives tend to need.

Title _____ Audience _____ Date _____

SETUP

YOUR STORY MAP

CONNECTION
Something that connects you and your topic to listeners.

CONFLICT
Either an obstacle or an opportunity that's relevant to your topic or book.

CONSEQUENCES
The natural result of the challenge, now or in the future.

POV
What's your point of view on this topic?

INVITATION (Starting)
How do you want listeners to think or behave DURING your talk?

PAYOFF
What do your listeners stand to gain?

Thank You Bubble

Set the itinerary

STORY

(First Stop) Chapter 1 *Title*

Information, details, and Spellbinders that further your Story

(Second Stop) Chapter 2 *Title*

Information, details, and Spellbinders that further your Story

(Third Stop) Chapter 3 *Title*

Information, details, and Spellbinders that further your Story

CONCLUSION

Thank You Bubble

POV
Reiterate your POV now that you've made your case.

INVITATION (Concluding)
How would you like listeners to think or behave AFTER your talk?

PAYOFF
What do your listeners stand to gain?

You'll notice that the Story Map has three main sections:

1. **The Setup** (or Introduction), which is comprised of the six segments at the top of the page.
2. **The Story,** which is comprised of the three chapters, as well as the information, details, and *Spellbinders* that support your point of view and convey your message.
3. **The Conclusion,** represented by the three segments at the bottom. The conclusion brings your story full circle.

The elements of this structure are there for you to use as organizational tools, but they become virtually undetectable to your listeners.

Every good story has a beginning, a middle, and an end: a Setup, the Story, and a Conclusion. It's as simple as that. In the following chapters, we'll work on the method for filling out the details of the map. It'll seem cumbersome at first, but in the long run it will abbreviate your process for preparing content going forward.

CHAPTER 5

Start Your Story Off Right with
the Perfect Setup

*"The simple truth is this, if our beginning doesn't do the job it needs to do,
the rest of your story most likely won't be read . . ."*
—Les Edgerton in *Hooked: Write Fiction That Grabs Readers at
Page One and Never Lets Them Go*

A talk, when it's at its best, is like a story. Not a memo. Not a data dump. Not a lecture. A story, written or spoken, needs to capture attention from the beginning, or people may not stay tuned for the rest.

Preparing the Perfect *Setup*

When I coach or conduct workshops, I spend the bulk of our content preparation time helping clients with the Setup, the introductions to their talks—and for good reason. It's in the beginning that most unskilled speakers set their talks in exactly the wrong direction. The first words you'll say deserve thoughtful attention. Not only does a strong beginning grab the attention of your listeners, it sets the tone and the intention of your message. If the beginning is prepared thoughtfully and with your goal and your audience in mind, the rest of the talk is far easier to design. Sometimes the rest of the talk practically writes itself because sorting out the Setup clarifies your direction.

When planning a prepared talk most speakers can readily name a bunch of things that they know they want to say, but it's in a jumble of fragmented ideas rather than a cohesive message or story. This is especially true of the Setup, during which speakers, out of nerves, excitement, or failure to prepare, often chatter without specific direction.

Many speakers start a talk by saying something like, *Hi, my name is_____, and I'm here to talk about _____, and thanks so much for having me, I know there was lots of traffic to get here, and Hi Mike, so nice to see you, and . . .*

If this was the first sentence of a book, would you read further? Me either.

A weak or rambling introduction creates the following problems:

- It fails to grab audience's attention
- It provides no focus or direction for the talk
- It gives the speaker a panicky feeling from which it's hard to recover
- It gobbles valuable time

A poor setup is expensive. A skilled Setup gives big payoff for the speaker and her listeners. It does what the name implies, it sets up the rest of the talk and it sets you up for achieving your objectives.

I propose using a frame for developing your introduction as part of your Story Map. Don't worry, though it provides a structure, your Story Map (and the Setup as part of it) will not come across as a canned template. The structure, if the story is well told, becomes undetectable as the story unfolds. Joseph Campbell's *The Hero's Journey* is an oft-used story structure, one most people are aware of as they read a book or watch a film. The *Hero's Journey* (and Martha Alderson's Plot Planner tool) can be used for comedy, sci-fi, tragedy, romance, adventure, literary fiction, or memoir. So, too, the Story Map can be used for a talk that is celebratory, humorous, inspirational, influential, or informative. Heck, I even helped a client use it to design the funny and heartfelt toast he was to give at his brother's wedding!

Prairie Dogging with Your Setup

When you're delivering a talk, you're competing with a lot of "noise" in your listeners' minds, bodies, and environments: their thoughts and emotions, the events of their day, their receptivity or resistance, their physical environment (too hot, too cold, too loud), their hunger, the discomfort of their chairs, and their vibrating smart phones. In the first few sentences of any talk, you want to cause an effect I call "prairie dogging."

Picture a prairie dog popping his head up from his hole to check out what's going on outside. He is intrigued, alarmed, amused, or curious about what is happening. This is what you want from your listeners. In the first few sentences of your talk—as well as at intervals throughout your presentation—you want to engage your listeners to such a degree that they mentally, emotionally, and sometimes even physically pop up, intrigued to hear what you have to say.

I call the first three statements (or sometimes questions) of the Setup the "C Level":

Connection, *Conflict*, and *Consequences*. These are the first three ideas (often spoken in just three to six sentences) that you'll use to start off your talk. The C Level is where you set the context for what you're talking about. It's also where you can achieve the "prairie dog effect."

Let's look at the C Level.

1: CONNECTION

The opening statement is one of *Connection*. It's usually a statement to which many if not all of those in your audience would respond by feeling "Duh," or "Of course." It can be positive or negative, but it is something that is generally understood. "These are crazy times," might be one example. It could be a statement of your excitement about being at the event. A connection could be a brief story that invites listeners to be able to empathize, even if they've not been exactly in the same spot. The Connection can be a shared sentiment, a universal truth, an undeniable observation, or a common experience. A statement of Connection often gets your listeners to nod in agreement. I'll offer more examples in a bit.

2. CONFLICT

The second statement is the *Conflict*. Good writers know that every story has conflict or it isn't much of a story. A conflict is not always a negative or combative thing in this context. Conflict for the characters we write can be (1) a challenge or obstacle or (2) an opportunity or goal. The conflict drives our characters to behave as they do through fictional or memoir stories. In nonfiction, the conflict is usually a problem faced or an opportunity to be seized by the readers.

The Conflict statement for speakers in this Setup is either an obstacle or an opportunity relevant to your topic. It gets your listeners to think "uh-oh" or "ooh." They're worried or excited, or at least intrigued. The Conflict statement is where you begin to reveal the stakes in the topic you're addressing. It might seem, at first, that you don't have a conflict to talk about at a book launch. The truth is, if you've thought about something long enough to write a book about it, there's conflict (challenge or opportunity) to be found. Obstacles and opportunities are always present in a written or a spoken story.

3. CONSEQUENCES

The third statement is the high-level (not detailed, yet) statement of the *Consequences* that spring from the Conflict. It's either a negative outcome that will, or has, happened because of the Conflict, or it's a positive outcome that can be missed if the conflict isn't addressed. This gets your listeners to think "yikes" or "wow."

Let's use Catherine Marshall-Smith's book launch message to illustrate a good setup.

CONNECTION

Recent events in our country have been deeply unsettling. Conflicts between politics and personal freedom are high. *(Duh)*

CONFLICT

My faith and my church have always been a source of strength for me. But now, my faith is being defined by vocal others who speak in direct conflict with my values. *(Uh-oh)*

CONSEQUENCES

My once soothing faith had become a barrier between me and the people I love, care about, and respect. *(Yikes)*

Notice that Catherine's C-level statements were born right out of the conversation that she and I had about her goals and the seeds for her book. She has launched right into her topic without a lot of yammering and throat clearing at the beginning. Her first statements are concise, clear, and to the point, requiring as little as a sentence or two each. Regardless of the political leanings of her audience members, their likely response to her opening Connection statement would be "duh," or at least nods of agreement.

Catherine had no need to introduce herself, she was introduced and her brief bio and the name of her book were part of the introduction. Lots of speakers, particularly at events that celebrate them or their accomplishments, start out their talks with a litany of thank-yous or a lot of other nervous jabber.

Catherine wasn't rude or ungracious. The Story Map contains two "Thank You Bubbles" that I'll cover later. There's time for good manners—even expressions of profound gratitude—once you've gotten the audience tuned in and engaged.

By doing this "C" level portion of the Setup, you've hooked the listener. You're right into the beginning, rather than chattering aimlessly. You've connected to your listeners. Their ears are perking up like adorable little prairie dogs. Now it's time to let them know where you're going with this talk.

The second line of the Setup establishes the purpose of the talk.

POV Is the Key!

As writers, you know that the point of view *(POV)* from which your story is told is one of the most important determinants of the tone and direction of your story will take. Who's telling the story? What does she think, believe, or know? What has he experienced? What is her bias? And most importantly, what does he want? The same is true for any talk.

The POV is the place to be bold! Of all of the elements of the Story Map, it's the POV that requires and deserves the most thoughtful consideration. Why? Because *everything* that follows the statement of your POV goes to support that statement.

The POV statement is the place where you get to declare your passion, your ideas, your beliefs, what you've learned, or your perspective on a topic. You can expose your heart, share your vantage, state what you know after your experience, or talk about what you hope for. The POV statement can be as big as *I believe if we don't change our current practices, we are bequeathing climate disaster on our grandchildren* (Al Gore). Or it can be as simple and lighthearted as, *I've come to embrace my own peculiarities as strengths, rather than seeing myself as weird* (J.P. Sears).

Your POV is where you expose your perspective, position, or state what matters to you. By sharing your POV, you expose your passion and your vulnerability.

Authenticity Matters

"The main thing is honesty. If you can fake that, you've got it made."
—Attributed to Groucho Marx, George Burns, Celeste Holmes, and others

The quote above may be clever and can work well for actors, but I don't advise it for speakers, particularly not authors. The most essential element of the POV is authenticity. This is the time when your voice becomes credible. Pick a POV statement that you can hold as your truth. Sincerity and authentic passion in appropriate measure to your topic are what will pull your listeners toward you as a credible voice. Your POV statement is simultaneously your strength and your vulnerability exposed.

Here are some examples of author POV statements I've made note of at book launches and other author talks:

"My background as a white woman from the American South gives me an onus of responsibility to tell the stories of the history of how black people have been treated in this country."
—Sue Monk Kidd, *The Invention of Wings* (historical fiction)

"I believe that animals are the most dependably reliable truth-tellers I've ever known."
—Pam Houston, *Sight Hound* (memoir-inspired fiction)

"99% commitment is a bitch. It gives you a possible out every single day. 100% is a far easier commitment to keep."
—Jack Canfield, original editor of the *Chicken Soup for the Soul* series, talking about his first *Chicken Soup* book (an anthology of inspirational essays) being rejected ninety-nine times before publication

"I'm really lucky I can write because I'm not much good at anything else. I'm guessing the rest of you writers might be like me."
—Anne LaMott, *Operating Instructions* (memoir)

"The power to speak and be heard was once reserved for only the most elite tribal leaders around the campfire. Today, our ability to record and distribute talks almost instantly and across the world has given us a worldwide campfire and everyone has the talking stick."
—Chris Anderson, "Head of TED," *Launching TED Talks: The Official TED Guide to Public Speaking* (nonfiction/how-to)

"Writing our stories is how we teach ourselves to be human."
—Cheryl Strayed, *Wild* (memoir/fiction/essays)

"I believe in love."
—Kate Perry, *Project Daddy* and more than twenty-five novels (romance)

These are all POV statements speaking in different styles about widely different books in a host of genres. The POV should be authentic to the speaker's view and in line with her goal for her talk. Some talks are controversial, with controversial POVs. Others are celebratory, with statements of gratitude as the POV. In any case, the POV statement deserves thoughtful reflection because it's the foundational piece of the entire talk.

The *Invitation:* Ask for What You Want

"If you don't ask, you don't get."
—Stevie Wonder, musician/songwriter

Every model I've ever seen for public speaking includes some kind of "ask" or "call to action." People often think of this only as an aspect of persuasive or sales-oriented talks. For author events, I prefer to think of this as an "invitation." It comes in two parts: the *Starting Invitation* during the Setup (introduction) of your talk, and a *Concluding Invitation*, a modified, more action-oriented version of it, during the Conclusion of your talk.

You can design your Starting Invitation for one or both of the following uses:

1. To give specific logistical requests (like turning off cell phones or holding questions until the end). I think of this as the "practical" stuff.
2. To prime listeners' imagination or emotions in order to welcome your ideas. I think of this as the more imaginative or even "trance-inducing" kind of invitation.

Let's look at some examples.

I like to think of the Starting Invitation as the beginning of a "trance" into which you're inducing listeners. If you're launching a book about how important it is to live a vegan lifestyle, the Starting Invitation could be something like, *I'm going to ask you to imagine yourself feeling healthy, strong, clear-headed every day, sleeping well at night, and being able to maintain your weight without effort.* Remember, the Starting Invitation is a request for people to think or behave a certain way *during* your talk. I think of the Starting Invitation as the "soft" invitation.

Don't misinterpret the term "soft" here. A Starting Invitation can be a powerful tool, particularly for controversial subjects. If we know there's resistance to an idea we are about to propose, we can use a soft invitation like this: *I know there are strong opinions on this topic. I'll ask you for a favor today. Just for the duration of this talk, I'll ask you to set your preconceived notions aside so that you can listen deeply to the stories and be open to an alternative to the view you hold.*

In a "trance-inducing" type of Starting Invitation we ask people to "consider," "imagine," "be open to," or "remember." We don't really deserve to ask them to go out into the world and act upon our POV here. Why? Because until we've delivered our whole talk, we haven't proven to them that our POV has merit; we have not *yet* made our case, nor earned the right (by presenting the content of our "story") to ask listeners to act differently.

As writers, we are natural creators of trances. Our stories are trances, a request that our readers suspend all else and enter into an altered state of reality.

Here are some imagined examples of Opening Invitations at author talks.

- *I ask you to think back to your own childhood and what you dreamed about when you were all alone.*

- *As I talk today, I'd like you to be open to the idea that everything you've ever been taught about saving money is wrong.*

- *Before we begin, I invite you to look around this room. What do you notice about the people gathered here today?*

- *Remember watching cartoons on Saturday morning, when you had only three channels and you argued with your siblings about who had to get up to change the channel?*

- *Sit back and relax while I take you on a journey to another galaxy where humans are the only species lacking the capacity for speech.*

All the hypotheticals above accomplish the same things: They request a receptivity of some kind, and they get your listeners thinking, feeling, or imagining something about the story you're telling—either the one you're speaking about, or possibly the one in your book.

But Why Should I? What's the *Payoff?*

When you ask someone—particularly a whole audience of someones—to do something, it makes sense to let them know what's in it for them. This is best stated after stating your POV and your Starting Invitation. What's in it for your listeners if they recall Saturday morning cartoons, or look around at the crowd, or relax and let you take them on an imaginary journey?

This is where you state to your listeners the Payoff for what you're asking them to do. Here are some possibilities:

- It's by recalling the most innocent of our childhood moments that we gain full appreciation for who we want to be as adults.
- Learning how money truly works will help you to have financial peace of mind with so much less effort.
- By taking the time to really look at who is around us, we can begin a new level of appreciation for just how diverse we are as a culture.
- Imagining other worlds is sometimes the very best way to gain understanding of our own.

Let's put the entire Setup together by going back to Catherine Marshall-Smith's talk. Remember her opening "C" level of her Setup. That's the top row on the Story Map.

CONNECTION

Recent events in our country have been deeply unsettling. Conflicts between politics and personal freedom is high.

CONFLICT

My faith and my church have always been a source of strength for me. But now, my faith is being defined by vocal others who speak in direct conflict with my values.

CONSEQUENCES

My once soothing faith had become a barrier between me and the people I love, care about, and respect.

Now, let's look at the second line of Catherine's Setup.

POV

I've come to believe that it's by looking at complex issues through a different lens that we can determine our real values. For me, that lens is faith and family.

INVITATION

Here's where I ask you to picture whomever you regard as "family." Are they all related to you? Or not?

I invite you to start thinking of "family" more broadly.

PAYOFF

By redefining family, we stand to gain a bigger harvest in our world. Validation. Belonging. Security.

When you read Catherine's Setup all together, you can see how it sets the tone as well as the topic of her talk. How much better is this than it would be to say, *Hi, name is Catherine, and I'm here to talk about the conflict between Christians and the LGBT community.* This kind of start would push a curious little prairie dog back into her hole!

At first, this process of sorting out the six parts of the Setup may seem laborious. It takes longer in the explanation (particularly in written form) than it does to design and deliver. Trust me, it gets easier and faster as you use this method, and it will ultimately prove not only to be a time-saver but an essential way to start every single talk. After preparing a few of them, you'll have the anatomy of the Setup in your bones. You'll be able to construct them in minutes, even on the fly for last-minute presentations.

Author clients of mine tell me that knowing the first words they're going to say for every talk when they're promoting their books is a huge comfort. Book promotion is exhausting and stressful. There's travel, logistical problems, jet lag, and stress. With all of that, it's comforting to know what you're going to say, particularly those first few sentences.

By setting the context, being candid about your perspective, and showing the value of your ideas to your listeners, you've hooked them right from the beginning. They're invested now. This is when they want to listen further.

Less is *Way* More in the Setup

While it takes me several pages to explain and demonstrate the technique for determining your best Setup, please know this: The *entire* Setup can take as little as six to twelve sentences to articulate. It is a vital portion of your talk, to be sure, but it should not take up too much of the time of your talk. For a thirty-minute talk, I'd say that the Setup should take somewhere between two and three minutes. If you're doing a two-day seminar, the Setup should take no more than five or six minutes. This is why the bulk of the prep time goes into the Setup: it needs to be both precise and concise . . . the trickiest kind of writing and speaking.

Developing a concise, engaging Setup, as well as practicing it so that it becomes automatic, keeps speakers from rambling and pulling too much into the introduction. If your talk is a grand house, the Setup is the foyer. You don't want the foyer to be filled with yard furniture, garden tools, bathtubs, and mattresses. Those things belong in the other rooms of the house. You want the foyer to be a crisp, welcoming entryway that invites visitors into the next rooms and sets the style of the home.

Speakers often put too much furniture in the foyer, diving into too much detail before they've set up the importance of the story. That's why they get redundant and lose track, and their talk turns into a list of stuff to say, rather than a cohesive, concise story. It's also why they so often run out of time.

The Setup Is Everywhere

Once you learn the elements of the Setup you'll recognize it in speeches, in debates, in religious sermons, in opening and closing arguments in court, in newscasts, in written op-ed articles and essays, and in advertising.

Think about commercials you've watched or heard on the radio, from an ad for medication to a luxury automobile to a late-night infomercial. Advertisers (from sincere product providers to tacky hucksters) have used some variation of the Setup since the first salesman plied his wares. Political and inspirational speakers and clergy use it, too, though usually in a more long-winded way.

We can even use the elements of a Setup in our intimate conversations with family members when we are making a case for our own idea. In my therapy practice, I've taught it to parents who used it to communicate their expectations with their teenagers. I'll even confess that I used a sweet, sincere, and tender Setup to get my husband on board for a trip to Italy a few years ago. Take a look:

CONNECTION
Honey, we've been talking for a long time about taking a really memorable vacation.

CONFLICT
I know money is tight and the idea of an international trip may not be in your thinking.

CONSEQUENCES
My concern is that if we keep putting these things off until the perfect time, a trip like this just won't happen.

POV
It's important for us to have adventures and shared memories and I think this is the perfect time for this trip.

INVITATION
Here's where I ask you to I'd like for you to be open to the idea and look at some of the money-saving ideas I've researched.

PAYOFF
By using miles and credit card points, without spending much more than a domestic vacation, we could have the trip of a lifetime together.

It was a lovely trip. Thanks.

I have no science for this, but my experience tells me that it is not knowing how to start our talks that causes a large percentage of our anxiety. I invite you to do the Make It Stick exercises below with the elements of Setup in mind. By truly learning this aspect of the Story Map, you'll be able to prepare your content efficiently and deliver it with confidence.

Make It Stick

 EXERCISE #1: MOCK UP A SAMPLE SETUP

"You can't be the kid standing at the top of the waterslide overthinking it. You have to go down the chute."
—Tina Fey, writer/comedian

Here's where I invite you to move the theory of this idea out of your brain, into your heart, and down through your fingertips. Before you go on to the next pages, take time here to really learn the Setup. A full understanding of the Setup will make the rest of the *Story Map* make sense. This is the *big deal* part of this tool, worthy of some lingering time.

To complete this exercise, I'd like you to pick a topic that you care about and might like to give a talk about. It can be a book launch, or a topic related to whatever you write, or even a mock talk that you could give trying to influence friends to take up a hobby you enjoy. Don't just "think" it, do this exercise with paper, pen, and Post-its. That's how you get it in your bones.

Pick your topic, then define your audience. Make it specific. This will help the learning process. Write answers to the four questions below to set your direction:

1. **Goal:** What do I hope to accomplish with this talk?
2. **Listeners' analysis:** What is my best assessment of who will be in the audience and what matters to them?
3. **Logistics:** How much time do I have to speak, and what is the setting like?
4. **Style:** What is the tone of the talk and the experience I want my listeners to have?

Use your answers and Post-its to create your Setup in the precise arrangement as on the next page. Experiment. Revise. Start over. Play. Here's a reminder of what the whole Setup looks like.

CONNECTION

Something that connects you and your topic to listeners. *(Duh)*

CONFLICT

Either an obstacle or an opportunity relevant to your POV (*Uh-oh* or *Ooh*)

CONSEQUENCES

The natural result of the challenge now, or in the future. (*Yikes* or *Wow*)

POV

What's your point of view, passion, or position on this topic?

INVITATION

How do you ask listeners to think or behave DURING your talk?

PAYOFF

What do your listeners stand to gain?

EXERCISE #2: TAKE YOUR SETUP FOR A SPIN

Use your smart phone or another recording device and speak your Setup aloud. See where your tongue trips or where the words start to flow naturally. Revise again, if you'd like, then record again. Trim if necessary. **Try it out until you can speak your Setup in two minutes or less.**

It's good to spend a bit of time honing your Setup. Though it's not the whole content of the talk, it sets the tone, the intention, and the direction of your talk. Filling in the main content of your talk is a whole lot easier with a clear Setup in the bag. That's where we'll go next.

CHAPTER 6

Design the Heart of Your Spoken Story

"Great stories happen to those who can tell them."
—Ira Glass, host of *This American Life* on NPR

Once you've determined your Setup for a presentation, you're ready to begin creating the main content. This is where the information, details, and *Spellbinders* belong. You kept the furniture—the details and information—out of the foyer. The "furniture" goes here, in the *Story* section of your map. This is the largest portion of your talk and where much of the detail takes place. All of it goes to support your POV.

Let's take a look at this middle section. It has two parts, the *Itinerary* and the *Story*.

Preparing and Sharing Your "Itinerary"

If you've ever taken children (or impatient adults) on a road trip you know they always want to know where they are on the journey. Laments of *Are we there yet?* and *How many more miles 'til we get there?* rise from the back seat.

Fair questions, in my estimation. Doesn't everyone on a journey like to know what the milestones are along the road? Don't they deserve to know how the journey is progressing and when they're reached designated landmarks?

The same is true for your listeners. Part of building trust with your listeners is establishing what the journey is going to be:

- Let them know where you're taking them (a mini-promise).
- Then take them exactly where you said you'd go (keeping the mini-promise, thus building trust and helping listeners follow along).
- Provide engaging surprises along the way (making the trip memorable).

Let's look now to the fattest content portion of your talk, the Story section of your Story Map. Once again, we'll use Post-its here. We're designing your flexible first draft.

The *Itinerary*, if it were part of a book, would be the Table of Contents. In a meeting, it would be the agenda. Given that I'm framing the idea of telling a story as taking listeners on a journey, the Itinerary is a list of the stops—in this case chapters—to which the journey will take listeners. The chapter names are titles. The information that follows each of them is the content of those chapters.

Why Three?

Notice that there are three chapters. Why three? Think of every nursery rhyme and fairy tale and a bunch of jokes that you know: three pigs, three bears, three guys go into a bar. Remember, you're telling a story. The pattern of threes is part of the architecture that nearly every culture has for listening to and absorbing stories, from our religious parables to our fairytales to our jokes. It's never *seven* guys go into a bar, and for good reason. Stories (particularly in the oral tradition) are sorted into threes because that's the easiest amount for people to retain and remember. It's a storytelling rhythm that we're accustomed to hearing.

If you're doing a talk of as much as an hour or two in length, three stops or *Chapters* are plenty for you to remember and your listeners to retain. You could use just one or two for a shorter talk of, say, thirty minutes or fewer. If you're doing a daylong seminar you may have four or five modules, but each module would have its own Story Map with up to three (rarely more) Chapters.

Determine Your Itinerary to Get Your Message "Down PAT"

I have never prepared a talk, or coached others in preparing theirs, when there was time enough to cover every single aspect of a subject or everything that the speaker knew about it. Time is finite. Attention is finite. That means that we can't dump everything into every talk; we must select, deselect, and organize. Here's the method for doing that.

Determining your three Chapters for a talk can be done in two ways, depending on your starting clarity on the topic:

OPTION 1

You already have an intuitive or logical idea of what they are and a natural order for them, for example:

- Past, Present, and Future
- Pros, Cons, and Decision Making
- The Lies, The Truth, and What We Should Do about It
- The Background of My Book, What I Learned about the Legal System, My Biggest Lesson (Catherine Marshall-Smith's three Chapters)

If you already have your three Chapters (categories) clearly in mind, that's great. If you don't yet know these, you'll use Option 2 below.

OPTION 2

The Chapters are not obvious to you. You have a bunch of things you want to say, but no structure in mind. In this case do what I'll call the P-A-T method, to get your message "down PAT."

The process when you're unsure of your Chapters is this:

- **P is for POPCORN:** Writing one idea per Post-it, brainstorm the ideas you'd like to include in your talk. Don't edit. Some of the items that you can count among your ideas are: information, exercises or interactions, stories, excerpts to read, demonstrations, fascinating details, examples, quotes, statistics, opinions, points you want to make, and so on.
- **A is for ARRANGE:** Arrange your "popcorned" ideas into families of things that go naturally together. This is a chance to eliminate redundant ideas. You may find that your ideas arrange neatly into three categories, lucky you. Or you may have more categories or a few straggler Post-its that don't seem to belong in a family. Reorganize and edit until you have three families of Post-its.
- **T is for TITLE:** Once you have your families, title them. These will become the Chapters of your story—the "stops" on your itinerary.

It'll look something like this:

Popcorn: Brainstorm in no particular order.

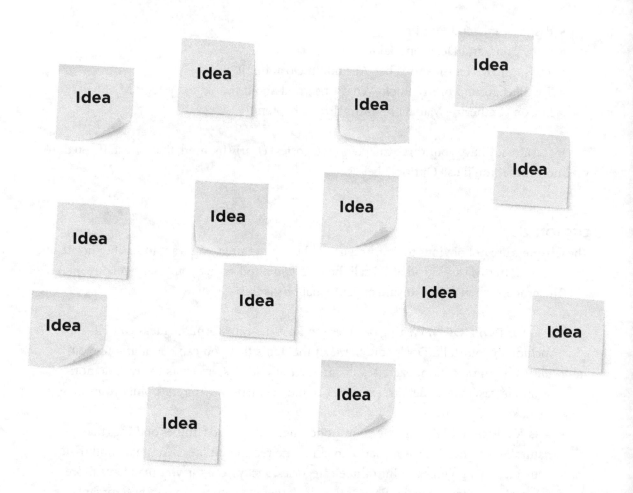

Just as with popping corn, you may find that you have a flurry of ideas popping all at once, then it dies down. Wait. Let a few more pop. You may even want to step away for a bit, take a break and come back to let a few more idea kernels pop. Generating ideas for a talk deserves a bit of reflection. Once you're satisfied that most of your ideas are written on Post-its, move on to the next step. Don't worry, if another kernel pops (and it's an important one) you can add it later.

Arrange: Organize the ideas into "families"—items that belong together. See if you can fit them into three families or groups that belong together. You may have a few orphan ideas that don't fit neatly into a family. That's okay for now.

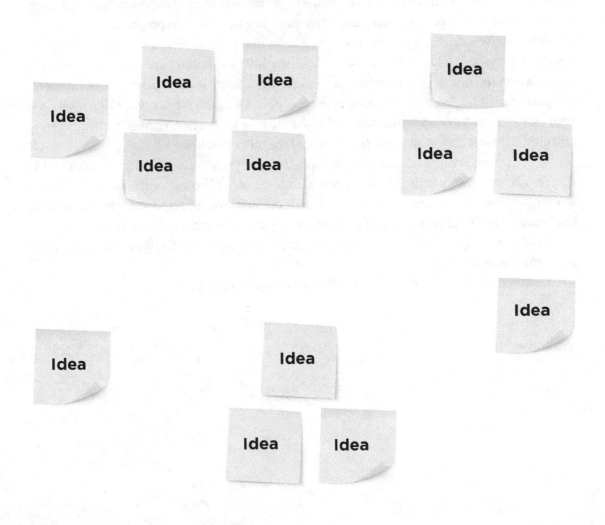

"In writing, you must kill all your darlings."
—William Faulkner

Far be it from me to disagree with William Faulkner but I don't think we need to *kill* all of our "darling" ideas when preparing a talk, or even when we're writing. When writing we must, however, select carefully among our ideas (and even whole scenes) and set some aside to either "kill" later or fit into another talk or a different written story. Sometimes these darlings don't make it into your prepared talk, but they can be answers to questions that may or may not come from your listeners. (More on Q&A in part 4.)

(A special side note, writer to writer: I edited out a whole section—fifty pages!—I'd written of my novel before publication, and with it one of my favorite supporting characters. I removed her, but didn't "kill" her. She's now a main character in a new novel in progress.)

After you've organized your brainstormed ideas into groups, you may need to re-evaluate your groupings and your individual ideas. You may notice that you have many more ideas in one group than another. You may have redundant ideas. Some Post-its may be standing alone, not part of any idea family. Take a look at those orphan ideas; are they crucial or extraneous to your topic? If they're crucial, you may need to shuffle your ideas again, arrange them differently, and eliminate less important ideas from some of the other families.

In our travel, in our writing, and in our speaking one thing is always true: we have to make choices about not only what to leave in, but what to leave out because our "journey" (whether written, spoken, or traveled) is finite and we can't do it all. We always have to choose between the "musts", the "mights" and the "if we have time" parts of any trip we're planning.

Don't move to the next step until you're happy with your idea families and you have no more than three of them.

I predict you'll catch my passion for Post-its doing this process.

Title: Give a title to each of the family groupings. Titles can be playful, serious, provocative, or simply labels.

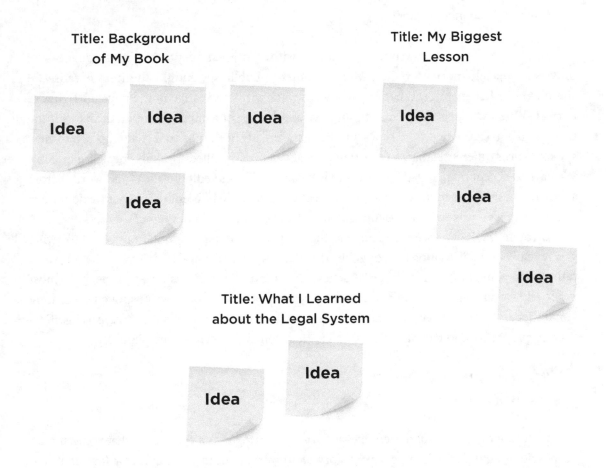

Once you've got your titles—the names of your Chapters in your story journey— and the ideas within them organized, you're ready to fit them into the Story Map. Here's where you as a writer—with a sense of story, pacing, and how to build to a story climax—have a gigantic advantage. The order should flow in a way that you can logically connect things, just like a story you'd write. More than being "logical," the Chapters and their contents should also be compelling enough to make your listener want to hear what's in the next one. In our writing, we want readers to read a chapter of our book and feel unable to wait to read the next. So too, as we speak the Chapters of our talks, we want listeners intrigued, excited to hear what comes next.

What to Keep, What to Chuck, How to Decide

"I'm not a very good writer, but I'm an excellent rewriter."
—James Michener, author

It finally dawned on me why so many writers—with all of their adeptness with language—are often an especially nervous bunch when it comes to public speaking. I think it's because we share James Michener's sentiments. We love to work with our words on the page until they're perfect. When we speak, it feels as though we are sharing our unedited rough drafts with the world and you can't edit a word or a sentence that's already been spoken. I challenge you to view spoken words differently than our written work. Even highly skilled speakers speak imperfectly. We have to accept that. Still, the process that I teach helps us to edit our ideas and words before speaking them, to get them as close to our ideal as we can. It's different than what we do for our writing, but it's a way to "rewrite" our spoken words before we share them.

Through the PAT process and beyond that, as you're honing the content of your talk, what you're really doing is writing the rough draft of the story you're going to deliver with your voice rather than your computer keyboard. I believe that one of the most basic reasons people—most especially writers—get stressed about public speaking is because once we've spoken something aloud there is no delete key, no chance to perfect what we've said. That alone, to me, is justification for preparing and having a method to perfect content efficiently and skillfully.

"My first drafts are a mess."
—Louise Penny, author

It's during the process of designing—and later practicing—your Story Map that you get to do the rewriting, editing, and honing of your story. Don't worry if the ideas are a mess at first. That's the nature of a draft, right? How do we decide what to leave in, what to leave out? What's essential? What's optional? What is a worthy embellishment that makes the story sing? What's a distraction from our topic or our goal? These are the questions every storyteller faces, whether writing or speaking.

The best advice I ever received about editing came from Sands Hall, author of *Tools of the Writer's Craft*. In a workshop I attended and in her book, Hall offered the perfect metaphor for deciding what to include and what to exclude from our writing. At the beginning of a book or a story, we are asking our readers to put on a backpack that they'll wear throughout the journey we're inviting them to take. Each character, each scene, each detail is a rock, a stone, or a pebble we're asking them to load into their packs. At the end of the story, our readers should feel that every rock, stone, and pebble they lugged was worth its weight.

As you sort through your "popcorned" ideas, as you determine your three Chapters, and later as you add colorful detail (which I'll cover in the next chapter), remember to look at each item on your map and decide if it's "worth its weight" in support of your POV and meeting your goal. Don't give a pebble a stone's weight, giving a minor item more time than it's due. Resist filling the whole pack with pebbles and nothing of substantial enough weight to make it a valuable part of the journey. Decide which of your stones are diamonds, small or large; we surely do not want to crowd out room for those with a bunch of plain old rocks.

Back to the Map

This is where the process of creating your message starts to gain traction. To arrange the middle section, the Story part of your message, you move the titles you just generated into the Chapters boxes on the left side of the map, and the supporting ideas of each, arranged horizontally to its right.

Play with them. Move them. Eliminate or rewrite them if they're not quite working for you. They're still Post-its and they crumple easily at your will.

Let's go back to Catherine Marshall-Smith's book-launch Story Map. After about thirty minutes generating ideas using the PAT (Popcorn, Arrange, Title) method, the middle of her map looked something like the model below. It had more words on each Post-it at first, but eventually she pared those down to about what you see below.

Remember, this is her map; she has to be able to read it while driving. The simpler it is, the better. This is the Story section of Catherine's Story Map. It takes place directly after her Setup.

Itinerary:

Background of My Book	Why I started this book	My crisis of faith	Writing to heal and learn Reading #1
The Court System	"Best interest of the child"= Farce	Children have no voice	Reading #2
My Biggest Lesson	Writing from an oppostition POV = insight	Summarize the conflict of the story	Invite Q & A

There's *No* Wrong Way to Tell *Your* Story

Here's the most beautiful thing about the structure of the Story Map: There is no right or wrong sequence, style, or content. The Story Map is a map of *your* thinking so that you can communicate *your* story in *your* style for *your* audience. It is infinitely customizable and begs for personalization. You get to arrange it as you like in a way that you find compelling. You are the author of this story.

You can start by reading an excerpt of your writing, or read one in the middle, or end with one. Some speakers want to hit the most important items first and build from there, while others want to build up to a big crescendo at the end. Just as in your books and stories, you decide the tone and the sequence of the storytelling. You select, deselect, and arrange the elements of your Story so that you are meeting your goals, all the while keeping your listeners in mind.

Catherine wanted to set the background of her story up first because her POV is to help listeners look at her book and her talk through the lens of faith and family. She wanted to do two readings from two different characters' perspectives—again in support of her talk's POV. And she wanted to end on an upbeat by talking about what she learned in the process of writing.

You'll determine the sequence and style of your talk. Arrange it until it feels natural to you and when it tells the story you want to tell in the finite time you have.

The Itinerary Calms Listeners—Keep Them Posted

After you've delivered your dynamic Setup, it's wise to let the passengers on your speaking journey know where they're going. This is where I list for my listeners a "fattened up" Itinerary for the trip we're taking together. For Catherine's book launch, we practiced her Itinerary and it came out something like this:

> *We're going to cover three things in this time I have with you today: I'm going to let you know a bit about the background of my book. Then I'll talk about what I learned about the legal system by sitting in a lot of family court sessions. And I'll share with you the biggest lesson I learned through writing this story. I'll read two short passages from the book and welcome your questions and comments at the end.*

Giving your listeners your Itinerary is the first promise you'll make to them. They relax, knowing that you're driving the car, you know where you're going, and they're happy to be passengers. When you arrive at each new Chapter (or Itinerary stop on your Story Map), let listeners know. For example, if Catherine is transitioning from Chapter 2, to Chapter 3, she could say something like: *Now that you've heard a bit of my story, I'd like to let you in on the biggest lesson I learned in writing it.*

Letting listeners know when you move to the next point on your map increases their trust. Subconsciously they feel as though you made a promise, and now you're keeping it. It can also serve to keep them from prematurely asking questions about a topic that they know you're going to cover.

If you're like me, you've been in a class or a lecture taking notes and the presenter says something like, "Now for my final point." And you think, *Wait a minute. What happened to the second point? Did I miss something?* Every second that your listener is wondering where you are in your Story is a second she's not listening to your story!

In the car, you want to let the kids know where you are on the car trip so that you can avoid the "Are we there yet?" questions. *Hey kids, here's the world's biggest ball of yarn I told you about. After this, we'll stop for lunch and the bouncy house.* The same is true of your passengers following your Story Map.

Keeping your listeners apprised of transitions is a way to keep their attention where you want it—on your content—rather than on wondering where you are in your story and if they've missed something.

Make It Stick

EXERCISE #1: DESIGNING THE STORY SECTION

For the same topic that you chose to complete a Setup in chapter 5, design the Story section of your mock talk, or more ideally, a real talk you intend or hope to give. Use Post-its and the PAT (Popcorn, Arrange, Title) method to determine your Itinerary and story elements. Arrange them on a Story Map, in the exact shape that I suggest.

By doing this exercise, you'll begin to see the real power of this tool for helping you to organize content for any talk.

CHAPTER 7

Add Spellbinders to Entrance Listeners

"Don't tell me the moon is shining; show me the glint of light in broken glass."
—Anton Chekhov, playwright

Every writer who has attended even one class or one writers' conference has likely heard the axiom, "Show, don't tell." In writing, as Anton Chekhov implies in the above quote, it is the sensory detail of a thing that will make an idea, action, or description clearer, more vivid, and more memorable.

A story that only "tells" is a list, not a story. The same is true of speaking. A list of facts or ideas is a data dump and not engaging or memorable. If we want to captivate an audience, we need to offer them vivid enough detail that they have an emotional, intellectual, or psychological response to it. This is the art of writing—and speaking.

"People don't remember what you say. They don't remember what you do. They remember how you made them feel."
—Maya Angelou, poet/author

The "showing" in a story is what draws us into it and lulls us into a trancelike state. You know this if you've ever been engrossed in a book or a movie and the ringing of the phone caused you to jump. The writer and the actors performing her script have cast a spell on you and you are under her power.

Spellbinders

After you've designed the story portion of your Story Map, I invite you to look at it again. Does it have color, sensory detail, emotional impact, and memorability? Have you been specific or general? Generic or personal? In other words, did you "tell," or did you "show" in some way by including specific, memorable details? (I'll again refer you to Sands Hall's *Tools of the Writers Craft* for specific information about showing versus telling.)

I call these details *Spellbinders* because they are a speaker's way of seducing listeners, capturing them under the spell of her story. We want them to forget what's out in the world and focus on what we're saying. That's a tall order; I know you're up to it.

"Your purpose is to make your audience see what you saw, hear what you heard, fell what you felt. Relevant detail couched in colorful language is the best way to recreate an incident as it happened and to picture it for the audience."
—Dale Carnegie, author

To create a trance, I suggest utilizing the following kinds of Spellbinders:

- **Specific mini-stories** (Short, on subject, and full of sensory detail. This could also be an excerpt you read from your book.)
- **Case examples** (if you need to prove a premise, a specific, detailed example)
- **Vivid statistics** (only true, relevant, and verifiable)
- **Relevant quotes** (Be sure you know the origin of the quote. They could ask.)
- **Audience interaction or activities** (from Q&A to practice exercises, to rhetorical questions that get people thinking, even if they don't interact verbally)
- **Humor** (*not* jokes)
- **Personal disclosure** (a true story from your own life that makes the point)
- **Metaphors, similes, and analogies** (to make complex simple or to make an idea that is vague more vivid)
- **Props and other visuals** (slides, white boards and flip charts, handouts, short video clips, or an object that you want to show or demonstrate)
- **Extraordinary language** (alliteration, turn of phrase, imagery, and so on)
- **Gestures and facial expressions** (that accent your content)

Many in this list speak for themselves. Let me clarify a few of them.

LANGUAGE AND LITERARY DEVICES

This, beautiful writers, is our ace in the hole.

Spellbinders can be funny, dramatic, startling, or poignant. I recall the TED Talk by Lidia Yiknavitch called "The Dream of Being a Writer." Her talk is solemn, raw, and honest. She talked of her lifelong longing to be a writer and said, "The dream of being a writer was like a small, sad stone in my throat." That line captured my imagination. It is vivid, visual, and artfully written, and she delivers it with a tone of voice and facial expression that is in perfect harmony with the agony of the statement. It was a perfect Spellbinder for its clear image and the poignancy with which it was delivered.

United States President John F. Kennedy uttered the now-famous words at his inauguration, "Ask not what your country can do for you, but what you can do for your country." That simple, elegant turn of phrase has retained its place in history because it was memorable and meaningful, but also because of the artful language used, saying a great deal with few words.

Many non-writers struggle with creating well-constructed language, never mind making good use of metaphors, analogies, and similes. We writers understand the impact of using these devices and clever turns of phrase. Metaphors, similes, and vivid language in speaking make your subject not only more memorable, but can make complex topics simpler and easier to grasp.

Neil deGrasse Tyson is an astrophysicist and author, and a frequent and fascinating guest on talk shows of every ilk. He has his own TV show called "Star Talk" as well. I invite you to do a search and listen to or watch some of deGrasse Tyson's talks. He is a magician at making the most enormously complex topics—space, infinity, string theory, the origins of our planet—simple and understandable to those of us without his scientific knowledge. He explains with stories, but also uses similes and metaphors that are within the understanding of average listeners. He's mesmerizing and wildly popular for this gift. I enjoy hearing him in any format, but prefer when he's a guest on a show speaking extemporaneously than when he's reading from a script on his own shows (though he's terrific at both).

You're not an astrophysicist, you say? (My apology to the one astrophysicist who may be reading this book.) Use deGrasse Tyson's example. Employ metaphors to make the complex simple, the unfathomable accessible, the important immediate, and the vague clear. Metaphors, similes, and stories are the best way I know to do this.

SLIDES

Many speakers begin preparation for their talks by immediately making a deck of PowerPoint slides. This is most true of my technology and business clients as well as nonfiction authors. Designing visuals before constructing your Story Map is that old cart-before-horse dilemma. It's rather like trying to put up wallpaper and laying carpet before you've built the walls of a home. I always recommend designing your Story Map *before* designing or determining any visuals.

Designing your story prior to creating visuals saves you time from the start. If you design visuals first, you could spend hours creating a slide deck and ultimately decide much of it doesn't fit into the story you want to tell. By designing a story first, with your goal and your audience in mind, you'll design only the visuals you need. What's more, your story should be able to stand alone with no visuals at all. Technology can fail, and often does.

Determine what you want to convey, then you can decide if a visual is necessary and useful. Clearly, if you've written a book on art history, photography, or economics and slides of art, photos, or charts are an essential part of your talk, you may use more visuals that the average author. Novelists and memoirists often require no visuals at all. That's okay.

TIP: One simple visual that I recommend every author have on hand is an enlarged image of her book's cover mounted on lightweight foam-core board. These can be large, if you're doing only local events, or small enough to slip into a suitcase. Posters of your book cover can be produced at your local print shop or office supply store. Typically, these are modestly priced and easy to carry. You'll use it at book launch events or on sales tables where you or others are selling your book. It also makes for a nice background for photographs at book events. When you post these, you are giving your book and its cover extra exposure.

VIDEO

Occasionally, a video can have a big Spellbinder impact and be worth the hassle. In general, a video should be relevant, short, engaging, and serve to illustrate an idea better than simply telling about it would be. Video projection is not always available in bookstores and other venues. Hotels and conference centers charge big bucks for video setup. Decide how important it is to you. Rock or diamond—you're always deciding which is which.

At the launch event for her bestselling memoir, *Dog Medicine*, Julie Barton showed a video clip about two minutes long as part of her talk. Her book is about her relationship with a special dog named Buckley and how training him and having him as part of her life was a crucial part of lifting her out of a profound depression in her early twenties. Julie showed the video of her initial training of Buckley. Seeing the simple activity and the relationship between them was emotionally engaging for the group and made the point far better than if she had simply described the process with words. Plus, we all got to meet (through the film) the spectacular Buckley! Definitely a Spellbinder.

PROPS AND DEMOS

Props can offer an unexpected surprise and serve as useful Spellbinders, even at a book launch. Patricia Dove Miller wrote a memoir called *Bamboo Secrets*. It's the story of her husband getting arrested while they were on an extended work visa in Japan (a bigger deal than one might imagine and a harrowing story). The setting and culture of Japan, and Patricia's experience of it, is a vital part of *Bamboo Secrets*. One of the cultural experiences she writes about is the ancient art of playing the Japanese bamboo flute. At her book launch, she read an excerpt from her novel, a scene about learning the flute, then brought her handmade bamboo flute out from a silk bag and played a short sequence for her listeners at the launch. It sounded primitive and complex all at once. This Spellbinder, in this case a demo, did the trick; it entranced the entire audience. I remember its haunting sound still.

My story, about searching through a loved one's home after his suicide, was published in the anthology *Shades of Blue: Writers on Depression, Suicide, and the Blues*. My story is called "In Search of the Silver Cup" and the whole story is about my desperate hunt for this little memento of my loved one's life. As I read the last few lines of the story at the anthology's launch event, I revealed the little cup and held it up for view. Several years after that reading, I still get letters and comments from audience members about the impact of the story and how glad they were to see the little cup at the end. They may have remembered the story without the prop, but I'm convinced that showing it made the story that much more memorable.

Just as with any element of a talk or a reading, I advise writers to use props and demos thoughtfully. They can be playful or profound, but should always be supportive of the POV or the reading, and not simply a gimmick or a distraction. They should not take up more time or hassle than they're worth. If they don't serve to help you meet your goal in your talk, they should be edited out. They can also be huge time gobblers, so don't give them more time than they deserve.

HUMOR, WITH CAUTION

"Humor is connective tissue."
—Holly Hunter, actor

Another commonly underused (and sometimes misused) Spellbinder is humor. When speakers get nervous, they can forget their natural senses of humor. They get stiff and somber while concentrating on their content and forget to be present. Humor requires presence. Of course, a serious tone in your talk is warranted if the subject matter is serious. Still, organic humor and spontaneous playfulness can be a natural part of most author talks and a welcome respite in otherwise serious talks. Those moments of humor, when we laugh together, are, as Holly Hunter said, "connective tissue" for you and your listeners.

Many people report to me that they've been advised to open a talk with a joke to warm up the crowd. This is the moment in my classes when I form my hands and face into the most begging, pleading, prayerful posture that I can and say, *"Please, use humor; do not tell jokes. I beg of you."* It is the extremely rare exception that a joke told as part of a talk is appropriate, non-offensive, and well-told. Most of us just can't pull it off.

Most jokes have some element of offensiveness and are therefore high risk. The jokes that we might feel comfortable telling in our closest circles—to the ones who know us and know our hearts—may not feel anywhere near as appropriate in a gathering of strangers. Jokes often don't translate well in multicultural groups. Many of us—even those of us with a great sense of humor—do not tell jokes well. We flub the punch line or forget the setup. A joke is a high-risk proposition. Stick with organic, natural humor.

Organic humor is particularly helpful during difficult moments. When that seagull pooped on my microphone during a talk (*I know, right?!*), I paused. Waited past my shock and disgust. Then I said, "Well, the reviews for this talk are already coming in." Everyone laughed and it was zero big deal. The host rushed to get me a clean mike. All good.

Humorous anecdotes, funny details, even laughing at your own flubs (oh . . . you'll have them) can serve as that "connective tissue" between you and your topic and your listeners.

AUDIENCE INVOLVEMENT

Audience involvement and interaction are among the strongest techniques for casting a spell on your listeners. Their participation can be verbal, an activity of some kind, or it can be mental/emotional and silent.

For a book event, you can engage interaction by posing rhetorical questions, asking the listeners to speak out an answer to a question, doing an exercise, or inviting Q&A. When you ask listeners to envision, imagine, or remember something, you're involving more of their senses than if you simply "tell" them something. Involve your listeners, or their attention wanders and the spell is broken. The more you engage their involvement (emotionally, mentally, physically), the more engaged they'll be.

Interaction and audience participation transform every presentation into a conversation, whether your listeners participate silently or by speaking.

I invite you to use every incantation in your writerly book of spells to captivate and engage your listeners. They'll be happy to be entranced by your capable magic.

Beware of Spellbinder Mishaps and Dark Magic

Here's the thing about casting spells; you have to make sure that they're going to get you the result you want. Anyone old enough to have watched *Bewitched* on TV, or those who enjoy the J.K. Rowling's *Harry Potter* books, knows that unintentional magic doesn't usually work out so well and that a poorly chosen spell can have disastrous results. The same is true for your Spellbinders. They should be chosen wisely. I'll use a political example to illustrate.

The United States 2016 presidential election was chock full of accidental Spellbinders on both sides of the race. Hillary Clinton meant to describe a fraction of the opposition's supporters when she used the vivid Spellbinder phrase "basket of deplorables." It stuck and caused a great deal of understandably heated opposition. Kellyanne Conway, a spokesperson opposing Clinton, used the term "alternative facts," which was so catchy (and contradictory) that it got lampooned on *Saturday Night Live*. Neither of these vivid bits of language served their speakers or their messages.

Because they're vivid and memorable, sometimes the only thing a listener will remember about a talk is a single Spellbinder. All the more reason to choose them thoughtfully. You want to cast the spell that supports your POV and engages your audience. You don't want to distract from your message with the use of "dark magic."

Make It Stick

EXERCISE #1: TUNE IN TO SPELLBINDERS

I challenge you to listen for Spellbinders as you watch or listen to others speaking, in your daily interactions, in the media, and in interviews on podcasts or on TV. Listen beyond the content of what they're saying for the creative and spellbinding ways in which they say it. Listen for metaphors, similes, and other literary devices. Watch for demos, case examples, statistics, and quotes or quotable turns of phrase.

EXERCISE #2: WHAT HOLLYWOOD KNOWS ABOUT SPELLBINDERS

When we think of your favorite movies or TV shows, perhaps even those we've not seen for years, certain moments stick in the memory. We may recall whole scenes. Anyone who's ever seen *Annie Hall* recalls the lobster scene, for example. Sometimes what we recall is a frightening, romantic, emotionally charged, or funny moment. Sometimes we recall only favorite lines from the movie that stood out and grabbed hold. These are the Hollywood version of Spellbinders.

In fact, years later, Spellbinders may be the only moments we recall about a film. It's good, as we're discussing Spellbinders, to know *why* a certain moment in a film sticks. In the selection below, from the American Film Institute 100 top film quotes of all time, ask yourself what it is about each line that makes it stick. Is it the words? The context? The delivery? The impact for the film? Or is it that it pulls for a certain emotional response: humor, fear, sentiment, intrigue, curiosity?

- "We'll always have Paris." (*Casablanca*)
- "Toto, I have a feeling we're not in Kansas anymore." (*The Wizard of Oz*)
- "I'm gonna make him an offer he can't refuse." (*The Godfather*)
- "I coulda been a contender." (*A Streetcar Named Desire*)
- "All-righty then." (*Ace Ventura, Pet Detective*)
- "Go ahead, make my day." (*Dirty Harry*)
- "I love the smell of napalm in the morning." (*Apocalypse Now*)
- "E.T. phone home." (*E.T.*)
- "Show me the money!" (*Jerry Maguire*)
- "Houston, we have a problem." (*Apollo 13*)
- "Mrs. Robinson, you're trying to seduce me." (*The Graduate*)
- "Snap out of it!" (*Moonstruck*)
- "I'm the king of the world." (*Titanic*)

Understanding why certain lines stick can give you insight into creating memorable Spellbinders in your talks. Plus, it's just fun.

CHAPTER 8

Stick the Landing with
a Compelling Conclusion

"The opposite of a happy ending is actually the unsatisfying ending."
—Orson Scott Card, author of *Ender's Game*

I love watching the summer Olympics, especially gymnasts. The skill, agility, and guts of those athletes astound me. I wait breathlessly to see if, after all of their aerial acrobatics, their landing will end in a single confident, two-footed touchdown or if they'll fall on their bums. I want to see every single gymnast stick the landing and feel a thrill each time they do.

I want the same for every speaker I coach and every writer who's reading this book. I want you to stick your landing and provide an ending that is satisfying to you and to your listeners. Once you've designed a dynamic Setup and a Story filled with compelling details and Spellbinders, it's time to look at how to stick your talk's landing.

Concluding Invitation

I have some good news about writing the Conclusion of your talk. Once you've designed your Setup and the body of your talk, the Story (which includes the Itinerary, Chapters, detailed information, and Spellbinders), the Conclusion is complete but for one small modification—the Starting Invitation must be redesigned as a *Concluding Invitation*.

Remember the lower row of the Setup at the top of the Story Map?

POV

(What's your point of view, passion, or posting on this topic?)

INVITATION (Starting)

(How do you want listeners to think or behave *during* your talk?)

PAYOFF

(What do your listeners stand to gain?)

Let's look at what it looks like at the bottom of the map, in the Conclusion.

POV

(What's your point of view, passion, or position on this topic?)

INVITATION (Concluding)

(How do you want listeners to think or behave *after* your talk?)

PAYOFF

(What do your listeners stand to gain?)

Notice that the POV and Payoff are the same in the Setup and the Conclusion. The Invitation is modified to reflect the difference between what we're asking of our listeners *during* our talk, and how we hope they'll act *after* hearing our talk.

The Concluding Invitation can be:

• **Practical for immediately following the talk.** *I'd love it if you all can stay to chat and enjoy some treats that I brought.* Or, *Please sign up on my mailing list if you'd like me to keep you updated about new books and events. Be sure to print your email address carefully.*

- **A way of thinking or an action to take out in the world.** *I invite you to look at "family" in a new way. I'd ask you as you walk around in your daily life to take notice of families around you. Notice what makes them family and how many different varieties there are.* (This was my own conclusion for my memoir launch.)

Use Your Conclusion to Your Best Advantage

"I just hate loose ends."
—Dan Brown, author

Too often when I'm listening to an author talk, the conclusion occurs simply because time ran out. That's not a fitting conclusion; it's a time management problem and it can drive a stake into the heart of a presentation that's gone well until that moment.

A skillfully crafted conclusion does more than end your talk—it makes the talk feel complete to listeners. It's a way to stick the landing by tying the Conclusion to the initial POV. In the Setup, your POV was just that, your point of view. Now, after delivering your Chapters, details, and Spellbinders, your POV has been validated, fleshed out, and clarified. You hope that it has also been understood and even embraced, though even the most compelling talk doesn't convince everyone. As you transition to your conclusion after delivering a stellar story, you can easily say something like:

Now you can see why I believe so strongly that . . ." or
I'm confident that you'll now agree that . . .

Then you reiterate your initial POV. It doesn't have to be word for word, but should be reminiscent in both content and language of how you stated your POV at the start so that people hear the "echo" and know you're coming around full circle.

Your Concluding Invitation is followed by an echo of the Payoff from your Setup.

By ending where you started, listeners automatically know that you're at the end. Think about how a certain musical theme might play at the beginning of a movie, then the action starts, and the story ensues. What happens at the end of the film? That same musical theme returns, an echo of the beginning to let you know that the story is coming to a poetic and intentional end. Listeners like to feel that they know where they are in your story while they enjoy little surprises along the way. By ending with an echo, they'll know you've come full circle. They'll know exactly where they are on your map—and so will you.

Time now for another of those mental shifts.

MENTAL SHIFT

Buy yourself room for error.
Though the content of your talk is all important, if you have a solid, tight, and dynamic Setup and you "stick the landing" with an echo in the Conclusion, the audience will be far more forgiving of small errors in the middle. In fact, they may not recall them at all once you've finished your talk with a solid ending.

CHAPTER 9

Gratitude Is Good:

Add a Thank-You Bubble or Two

*"To speak gratitude is courteous and pleasant, to enact gratitude
is generous and noble, but to live gratitude is to touch Heaven."*
—Johannes A. Gaertner, author, art historian

The quote above is among my longtime favorites, and reflects a great deal of how I hold the value of gratitude. I believe that gratitude is an essential element of a rich life and should be a part of all of our exchanges, both private and public.

Gratitude is an important element of humility. Many speakers confuse self-deprecation for humility. Humility—and gratitude as part of it—elevates your listeners. It says "we're all equal". Excessive self-deprecation says, "I'm less than". I much prefer a humble speaker to a self-critical one.

Still, even our expressions of gratitude should be intentional parts of our talk and should find their appropriate places in our Story Maps. Expressing our sincere gratitude during speaking events can be not only gracious, but a sincere and touching element of any talk. Done poorly, insincerely, for too long, or in the wrong spot in your talk, thank-yous can cause your presentation to go flat and, worse, can reduce the trust your listeners will grant you.

Given that many author talks are either readings or book launches, I've included a little feature on the Story Map that I call the *Thank You Bubble*. Often at book launch events, particularly when they take place in their hometowns, authors like to thank their hosts and friends and loved ones who came to support the event. This is good. Have some fun! Just remember your goal for the talk and give your appreciations only the amount of time that you can afford within the timeframe you have.

A bubble isn't a fixed feature. The Thank You Bubble can float to where it works best in your talk. Too often I hear new authors at their book launches spend the first five minutes thanking a list of people known only to a few in the audience. I'm all for manners and gratitude, but placed there, right at the start and for too long, you run the risk of drowning your audience in the thank-you pool.

What I advise doing is a super-short, super-sincere thank you at the start. Something like, *Wow, I'm overwhelmed to see so many friends and loved ones here. Thank you, Mary, for that wonderful introduction and thank you to this fabulous bookstore for hosting this event.* Then you go on with your Setup to get the listeners into the topic.

If you have a longer list of specific thank-yous to offer where you're naming people in the room (and you may not if you're in a room of strangers), I advise saving those more detailed appreciations (the Thank You Bubble) for directly after the Setup. You can do it right before or right after giving your Itinerary, or you can build it in as part of the last of the Chapter of your talk and as a transition to the Q&A. If you're in your hometown and have lots of loved ones and writing pals at your launch, it's fine to list a few, of course. Just keep it simple and mind your time.

Note that I added a second Thank-you Bubble toward the end of the Story Map. Also note that it is a smaller bubble. At the end of your talk, before you move to your Conclusion *and* as you are about to wrap up, it's reasonable to say (even to repeat) a brief appreciation to your audience for coming and your host for having you.

CHAPTER 10

Practice Makes Nearly Perfect

~⌒∂

"Everyone rehearses. Some people just do it in front of an audience."
—Unknown

For those of us not prone to think of ourselves as performers, the idea of "rehearsing" may feel peculiar. Speaking your whole talk aloud for the first time, in front of an audience, is fraught with peril. Without rehearsal, you have no idea how long your talk will actually take. (It's likely longer than you think.) Without rehearsal, you don't know which words will trip your tongue, which ones are hard to recall, and which ideas just don't sound right. Practicing your talk aloud will give you information you cannot get by practicing silently.

"Be sincere. Be brief. Be seated."
—Winston Churchill

Practice Aloud

Practicing out loud gives you a sense of flow of your story, where it's flat and needs a Spellbinder to juice it up, and where it's powerful. It'll give you a more realistic sense of timing for each item you're including. I'll admit that rehearsing aloud felt odd to me at first. It's now an invaluable part of my preparation for important talks. Every time I omit this step, my audience gets what is much more akin to a rough draft of my talk than an edited, polished address. If your talk is important to you, if the stakes are high, or if the content is new, I strongly suggest practicing it aloud.

Some speakers rehearse, but with an ineffective method. They look at their notes, then close their eyes and mentally mumble the components of their talk. Not only is this silent method ineffective, it tends to make your talk more confused and adds more to your nervousness. Why? Your brain can generate far more words in a single second than you can articulate in thirty seconds or even thirty minutes! If you practice only silently, you'll be "popcorning" more ideas every time rather than focusing. Practicing aloud will help you trim, edit, and tighten your talk, as well as quell some of your nerves.

Practicing only mentally and without speaking the words would be like a pianist rehearsing without touching a keyboard. Your voice is your instrument. It's only when you speak the components of your talk aloud that you'll hear where it works and where it doesn't. Just as a dancer preparing for a performance rehearses to put his steps into "muscle memory," it's vocal rehearsal that gets your story "in your bones."

Memorization versus Spontaneity

"Spontaneity is an infinite number of rehearsed possibilities."
—Peter F. Drucker, philosopher/author

Please note that I am not recommending that you *memorize* your talk as though it's a script. In fact, that's a method reserved for only the most formal of events. Remember that the Story Map is a hybridized tool, ideal for both preppers and pantsers. The preppers design their map so they can recall their talk, but are not frozen and stiff from over-memorizing it, and they appear more spontaneous. Pantsers can have impromptu additions, but their map keeps them from letting their spontaneity cause them to drift too far off of course without meeting their goal.

Everyone I know has a handful—some have a huge handful—of stories that they've told a hundred times. Sometimes siblings or spouses chime in with their familiar part of the story you're telling. These are the stories you pull out at gatherings of friends, at family holidays, and in the workplace. Though they may be stories you've told a hundred times, to your listeners (at least the ones who haven't heard them before), they sound spontaneous. You hone the story over time and with repetition, hopefully in front of different audiences. You learn which parts captivate, which details to include, how to create suspense, which parts get the laugh or the *aww* or the *yikes*. You know this because you've repeated the story. That's all. The same is true when you have a talk to give. Repetition helps you not only to learn your talk, but to do it so well that you can speak it with ease and in a fascinating way.

The paradox is this: You practice a talk or a story so that it sounds more spontaneous.

Is It Perfect?

"There are always three speeches for every one you actually give. The one you practiced, the one you gave, and the one you wish you gave."
—Dale Carnegie, author

What Carnegie implies in the quote above is that we must accept that any talk can be improved upon, and that none of them go precisely as planned. Again, we writers like to revise our words and get them perfect! When we speak live, there's no delete, no find-and-replace. *All the more reason to practice.* The more times you deliver a presentation off your lips, the closer the finished talk will be to the one you prepared, and you'll travel home with a lot fewer regrets.

With preparation and practice, the differences between the "three speeches" that Carnegie talks about can be much smaller. Not perfect, but as close as possible, with reasonable flexibility for in-the-moment interactions and spontaneous exchanges with your listeners.

I find comfort in another speaker's words:

"I'm like a recovering perfectionist. For me, it's one day at a time."
—Brené Brown, author

If I had my perfect druthers, I'd ask every speaker to record her rehearsals, listen back to them for smoothness, good transitions, and timing. The higher the stakes of our talk, the more seriously we should practice it.

If you practice only part of your talk—though I recommend practicing the whole thing—I advise that it should be the Setup and the Itinerary. Speaking your Setup aloud four to five times will make an enormous difference in your confidence. It's only a couple of minutes long, so worth the time. Practicing the Itinerary aloud familiarizes you with the direction of the journey you're taking your listeners and gives you a mental map of where you're going. With this in place, you and your listeners can relax and enjoy the trip.

CHAPTER 11

Make Revisions and Create *Useful* Speaker Notes

"The only kind of writing is rewriting."
—Ernest Hemingway, author

As you practice your talk, you'll get a sense of which pieces of it work, which need tweaking, and which can be chucked completely. You'll hear redundancy. You'll hear gaps. Your Story Map is still made of Post-its, so it's easy to make course corrections. As you practice and revise your map, you're also in the process of creating your one-page speaker's notes, should you want to use them. Revision is just as important in speaking as it is in our writing. I much prefer a one-page set of notes to a set of index cards, or worse, a stack of paper stapled at the corner that you have to flip through as your notes. It's too easy to get flustered or disoriented when you're nervous or excited. The Story Map is not only a method for preparing your content, but for preparing your notes as well.

Revisions

This is where you should trim the number of words per Post-it. The better you know your talk, the fewer words (and simple images) you'll need to jog your memory as you speak. Remember, the map you're making here is not a detailed atlas, but a simple roadmap you can read while on your course. You want to be able to glance at your notes and pick up what you need. I'll address some techniques for using your notes when I address delivery skills in part 3, but for now know this: Simple words and even simple images (like arrows, dollar signs, or other graphics that help to abbreviate) on your map will make it much more usable. You wouldn't write, *Turn left at the big red barn with the painting of a giraffe on it* on an actual map. You'd probably write *L @ Giraffe Barn*.

Simplify your notes with just enough detail that you can recall what you prepared to say and not so many words that you'll not be able to read them quickly.

Oh, and print legibly. You'll curse yourself if you can't read your own writing.

Look Out for Over Packing

Having traveled extensively for personal and business purposes, I've learned one important thing about my process of packing a suitcase: The more last-minute I pack, the more likely I am to over pack, to pack the wrong stuff, or to forget to pack something important. If I'm flinging items into my suitcase just before departing, I'm likely to end up with five pairs of black shoes, no toothbrush, and without my phone charger. (How many chargers have I bought in airports?!)

The same is true of assembling the components of a talk. While the Story Map can be used for last-minute (even mental) prep for a spontaneous talk, that's not how I recommend using it when you have advance notice, when the stakes are high, when the content is new to you, or when you're especially nervous. Designing your Story Map well ahead of time allows you to evaluate, trim, and get the talk tight as well as giving you a realistic assessment of the duration of your talk.

My rule of thumb is this: Plan content for no more than about two-thirds of the time you're given to speak. For a thirty-minute talk, I prepare twenty minutes of content, max. For an hour, I prepare about forty minutes. Even if I deliver my talk perfectly, without redundancy, the additional time can be reserved for Q&A, playful interaction with listeners, and the occasional spontaneous addition. No one will get mad if you end a bit early, though you likely won't.

Preparing and delivering content for a public talk reminds me of shaving cream. You push the can's button and a dab of white foam comes out in your hand, but it doesn't stay that size—it expands. That's what happens to spoken content due to nerves, delays, interruptions, and audience interactions. Don't over pack—your content will likely expand.

Time for a quick mental shift.

Here's a direction you'll never be given: *Don't worry about time at all. The audience has infinite patience and absolutely nothing to do but hear every thought you've ever had about this subject.*

You'll always have to select and deselect what is possible to talk about in a given time frame. And yes, you'll nearly always have to leave out important things in favor of more important things. That suitcase is only so big.

Revising and Paring It Down

As you rehearse, you'll likely revise some elements of your talk. That's great. The Post-its come in handy for this. You may re-order your Chapters, add Spellbinders, or cut out items that are either redundant or not as necessary as others.

Do be cautious. There's a temptation during rehearsal to keep stuffing the suitcase with more and more detail. You'll have to fight the urge to over pack during revision.

A One-Page Snapshot

One of the bonus features of the Story Map method, as opposed to writing a script or even an outline, is that the process of creating your talk also results in a one-page snapshot of your whole talk. I've seen too many speakers holding a stack of index cards or waving around a stapled stack of papers that they have to leaf through as notes during their talks. Not only does this look sloppy, it is also highly ineffective.

I witnessed one speaker—yes, an author at her book launch—drop her stack of index cards and watch them flutter to the floor like so many autumn leaves. I'll never forget the look of abject terror on her face. She became unraveled for several minutes while audience members gathered her cards and handed them to her, hopelessly shuffled, and useless. It threw her off so much that she appeared a little shell-shocked for the rest of the talk.

Story Map as Mind Map

I strongly recommend that you use the Story Map, in its exact shape, for every talk. The components and their locations on the page will become etched in your memory. You'll also internalize the shape itself. If I'm a bit lost in the content of my talk when I'm delivering it, I often don't need to consult my notes. I simply pause and the whole image of my map pops into mind, not unlike being able to close your eyes and envision exactly where a specific item sits in your refrigerator. A single page is far better than shuffling through a deck of cards or sifting through a stack of paper.

I like to photocopy my Story Map with the Post-its on it so that it's flat and I don't risk one of my Post-its falling off. Ideally, I make a color copy. I also like to scan my completed maps, and file paperless copies of them on my computer. I may pull that map out for use another time down the road. Maybe I'll use the whole map as is, or I'll revise a bit by placing a new Post-it over the top of a photocopied one to revise the talk for a new audience or to update the material for any reason.

You'll be surprised how versatile this tool can be.

Color Is a Good Crutch

I offer one completely optional tip for creating the final version of your notes vis-à-vis the Story Map. When my map is how I like it, I often use a second color of Post-its (often a neon shade) to stand out from the pale yellow ones. I use the neon to remind me of highlights I don't want to miss, or to indicate where I'm using a visual. I often use a special color for my Thank You Bubble. Whatever works for you. I sometimes use brightly colored paper to offer more contrast with the light yellow Post-its and find it easier to read at a glance.

Make your notes as useful to you as you can, but resist cluttering them up with too many words or dozens of extra items. Don't layer Post-its such that you'll need to peek under them to get your idea. Remember, you're driving—your map should be readable at a glance. You'll often find you don't need notes at all, but when you do, I recommend the K-I-S-S method: *Keep it simple, sweetie.*

Below is a photograph of the Story Map notes I used for my own book launch of my memoir, *Filling Her Shoes.* I posted yellow Post-its on darker paper (blue in this case) because I find it easier to read that way. Whatever works for you is okay. By preparing your content in this exact shape every time, it's a little bit like always putting your keys in the same place so you'll always know where to look for them. By using the Story Map in its exact shape, you also internalize it so that future maps take less and less time to prepare. With the "mechanics" of preparing your content kept uniform, you can focus on the actual content.

A Super-Duper Extra Story Map Bonus for Writers

The Story Map is not just a tool for developing a talk. It can also be a magnificent method for organizing nonfiction content for books and articles.

If you're sending an email that is meant to influence others, you can use the map to organize it. It can be a frame for an agent query, the shape of a how-to article, a political position article, or anything else that imparts information or is meant to motivate an attitude or action.

The map can be the outline for each chapter in a nonfiction book. In fact, this whole book has been written using the Story Map as my frame for each of the major parts, and a cascade of Story Maps for bigger subtopics under each. Book-length writing entitles you to take some liberties with the model, of course. Having more than three chapters is necessary for most books, but the basic frame is the same. Throughout this book, you'll find Setups, Itineraries, Spellbinders, and Conclusions, just as I'm teaching them throughout part 2. A non-fiction book like this one is simply a fattened up story. A fattened up Story Map is the perfect tool for developing it.

Here's a photo of the Story Map I had in my office on a bulletin board during the writing of this book. I used index cards instead of Post-its. For a book-length "story" I afforded myself a few liberties, including having more than three main "Chapters," but the basic structure is the same. As I wrote, I referred often to my map to keep on course. In the writing, I added, changed, and reorganized a bit, but this was the starting point.

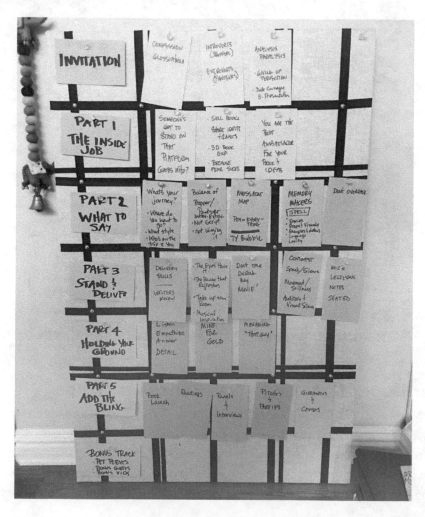

BONUS TIP: This method of using large Post-its or index cards on a larger surface (a wall or a bulletin board are examples) is also great if you're planning a talk with a partner or a group. To work out your Story Map together, then divide up who is going to say what is a much better strategy than designing the talk separately, without a cohesive, shared story.

Conclusion to part 2

When it comes to building content for a talk, I urge you to recognize the huge advantages and assets that you, as a writer, bring to the experience. While writing is different than speaking, its primary difference is in the delivery of the content, not in the elements of the content itself. By using the literary devices that writers already have in their pockets, and coupling those with the Story Map as a repeatable structure, writers are positioned to be exceptional speakers.

Experiment with the Story Map. It'll feel like a pair of stiff jeans at first, but when broken in, I predict it'll become as comfy as a favorite pair of old sweatpants.

Now that you know the components of the map, listen for them, look for them. You'll find them in commercials, TED talks, news reports, political speeches, and in articles. They'll be sophisticated and amateur, elegant and tacky, smooth and clunky. The components may be arranged differently, but you'll begin to see what an organic process it is to build a talk with these elements. I predict—and with a great deal of authority after witnessing it so many times—that if you use the Story Map five times, you'll fall in love and you'll use it for every talk you deliver.

Next up, we'll switch away from content and move on to the delivery skills of public speaking, because it's not always about "what you say," but also "how you say it" that can determine the impact you have on an audience.

Before you move on, I invite you to do the following exercises.

Make It Stick

 EXERCISE #1: DESIGN YOUR OWN STORY MAP

1. Using the Post-it technique and the Story Map template, create a talk of your own. Perhaps it's an actual talk you have scheduled, or you could use the Story Map to redesign a talk you've given in the past.
2. For fun, you could choose a favorite book by another author and pretend you're launching that book. How would Harper Lee launch *To Kill a Mockingbird*? How

would John Steinbeck launch *Grapes of Wrath?* J.K. Rowling launching *Harry Potter?* How might Xaviera Hollander have launched *The Happy Hooker?* At this point it's all about learning the tool. Play with it. Have some fun. Experiment!

3. Once you've designed your map, try recording yourself delivering the talk, particularly the Setup. Listen back, make changes, and re-record. I am confident you'll find that your talk will improve with each rehearsal.

   EXERCISE #2: BECOME A SKILLED OBSERVER

1. I find that once my clients learn the components of the Story Map, they recognize it all around them. Sometimes it is skillfully used, and sometimes not so much. I invite you to have pen and paper in hand when you listen to a TV ad, watch a TED talk, listen to a sermon, take a class, or attend a writers' event. See if you can identify the map components and make note of them. Listen especially for the POV and the Invitation, and observe your own reaction.

2. Do an internet search for Abraham Lincoln's Gettysburg Address. The entire speech (it's not as long as you might remember from school) is an example of an extended (and eloquent) Setup. Print it out and label the elements of the Setup. It's a way to see how timeless these features are.

3. Pay attention, in your daily interactions, to when others are using elements of the Story Map. It could be your kids pitching for a privilege they want. It could be your boss announcing a new policy or procedure. Make mental note of the elements and effectiveness of their pitches and announcement.

 EXERCISE #3: VIDEO VIEWING

1. Ashley Graham is a model and "Body Advocate." Watch her TED Talk, "Plus Size? How About My Size?" Take note of the following:

   • What is the speaker's POV?
   • What is the invitation she makes to listeners?
   • What are her Spellbinders?

- What did you think of her use of the mirror as a prop and as her Connection at the beginning of her talk?
- What might you have added or done differently if you were delivering the same talk on the same subject?

2. Shonda Rhimes is a renowned creator and writer of popular TV programs. Her commencement address to the graduates of Dartmouth in 2014 will give a boost to any hesitant speaker. It's a bit long, but worth a listen for some inspiration.

- Note that in Rhimes's address that the Thank You Bubble, as is tradition for this kind of talk, takes place in the first moment of the talk. What's your response to that? Does it work in this setting? Would it work for a talk you deliver?
- What are your take-away nuggets or inspirations from Rhimes's talk?
- What were her Spellbinders? Her POV?

3. Do a search for any video of Neil deGrasse Tyson speaking.

- Watch his use of analogies, metaphors, and simple stories to communicate complex ideas.
- Observe his animation and passion for his subject, particularly when he's in interviews, speaking extemporaneously (though he's always fascinating).

PART 3

How to Say It: Stand and Deliver with Simple Skills That Make All the Difference

"A blur of blinks, taps, jiggles, pivots, and shifts . . .
the body language of a man wishing urgently to be elsewhere."
—Edward R. Murrow

We've all been here. We sign up for the class or workshop, or attend the breakout session at a conference excited about the topic and what the speaker has to say. Then she begins her talk and we can barely hear her. She's talking to the floor in front of her, hardly looking up. People holler out, "Can't hear you!" and she adjusts her volume for a second or two then resumes her nearly inaudible talk. Or we can hear her, but her constant tugging at her clothing, or fidgety hand movements, or repeated throat-clearing, or pacing (maybe all of them at once), make it hard to listen to what she's saying. The session just started and we are already looking for the door, wondering if we can discreetly slip into another talk.

Despite our interest in the topic and the speaker, the way she's delivering her talk overshadows the content she's sharing. It's not *what* she's saying, but *how* she's saying it that is the problem.

The writers I've coached for speaking events seem especially focused on the "what" they're going to say, and don't think to invest attention in learning the skills of "how" to say it. I get it—we are word people, but there's more to a presentation than the words.

Delivery skills—what you do with your face, hands, voice, and body—do not replace your expertise or your story. However, poor delivery skills can prevent listeners from hearing your message at all or, worse, can keep them from wanting to hear it. By the same token, great delivery skills, while they don't replace poorly prepared content, will enhance your story, make it more vivid for your listeners, and add a layer of fascination about you and what you have to say. Skilled delivery enhances your content. Perhaps most importantly, good delivery skills techniques are simple and highly learnable.

Think back to classes or talks you've attended. Think of one that was dynamic and engaging and another that was either uninteresting or off-putting. Can you picture each speaker? Can you recall what you liked or didn't about each talk? Some of your response could be about the content, but I'm betting that much of your experience (and memory) of a speaker is *how* she delivered her content and how it made you feel—amused, startled, concerned, inspired, informed—not the content alone.

By learning a few simple delivery-skill techniques, you can instantly enhance your engagement with listeners, add dynamics to your content, and, at the same time, manage and reduce your anxiety level without your audience even knowing what you're doing.

Here, I'll break down good delivery skills and offer the techniques that I offer all of my clients. It's tricky in written form to describe delivery skills, so I'll provide suggestions for viewing examples and practice exercises.

On a separate note, I invite you to notice that you've just read a Setup and an Itinerary to introduce part 3. There is a Setup at the beginning of each new part of this book as well as for many of the larger chapters. And now, our Itinerary for part 3. . .

In part 3, we'll cover:

- Bringing your most natural, best self to every presentation
- Using Cool Composure and Warm Energy: simple delivery skills to set the right "temperature" for every presentation
- Tips for using microphones, lecterns, visuals, and notes

CHAPTER 12

Bring Your Most Naural,
Best Self to Every Talk You Give

～⁰

"I don't like being in front of people [as myself].
In character, I could get up and talk for half an hour."
—Kristen Wiig, comedian/actor

Creating Your Confidence

In part 1, we talked about the "inside" work: attitudes, assumptions, and mental shifts that can help ready you for speaking in public. As much as I believe in the benefits of shifting our thinking—as is evident from how much type devoted to it in this book—I want to share a little secret with you in this quick mental shift followed by a video example.

MENTAL SHIFT

You can create confidence, energy, and composure from the outside in.
Adopting a confident body posture and bold movements and gestures invites confidence. Assuming relaxed posture and body movements calms you. "Acting" calm helps you to feel calm. "Acting" energetic (even if you're feeling a little low-energy) invites energy.

   Just as dressing a certain way can affect our mood and attitude, so too can "putting on" delivery skills. Don't wait for confidence and energy; put them on— like clothing—and they'll arrive within you. If I'd delayed speaking until I felt fully confident in my abilities to speak well, I'd still be waiting.

Amy Cuddy addresses body language in her books and her talks. She examines body language both for what it says to others, and for what the position of your body does to your own disposition and emotional experience of a moment. I invite you to take a look at her TED Talk, "Your Body Language May Shape Who You Are," prior to reading the rest of this section. Seeing her examples, then reading my ideas will help you to "see" what I'm saying. Take a look.

Inside Out/Outside In

Now that you're watched Amy Cuddy's talks—you really did, didn't you?—I'm going to ask you to hang with me here because I'm going to share two seemingly contradictory, nonetheless, truthful ideas.

First, as Cuddy's message conveys, we can "put on" our confidence and other sensations by altering our outward behavior. I do this all the time. I've delivered highly energetic talks while ill, jetlagged, and otherwise exhausted. By using the energy skills I'll talk about in coming pages, I can raise my energy level. The same is true in reverse. If I'm anxious, jumpy, or feeling wildly nervous, I can "put on" the skills of composure and find that I can calm myself. I always encourage people to be "authentic" in front of groups, to be themselves. It's just that I want to be my "best" self—not my sick, tired, anxious, out-of-my-mind self. It's true, then, there is a little of the "fake it 'til you make it" in the idea of "putting on" confidence or calm as if they're clothing. I can live with that. To me this is not being inauthentic or a false self. It's more like being my best self, akin to tidying my house before guests arrive.

Still, by asking you to *invite* confidence, energy, and composure, by changing how you're using your body, I am not asking you to be false or to be a performer.

The single biggest *aha* I had that transformed me from being glossophobic—utterly terrified of public speaking—to having the courage, confidence, and desire to stand in front of an audience of any size was this:

Audiences don't want a performance from a speaker. They want an authentic, meaningful connection to the person who is speaking and his message.

I was under the misapprehension that public speaking was a performance and that since I am no performer I could never be a skilled speaker. What I didn't know was that the very best speakers are those who appear the same when they are speaking at the front of the room as they do when having a one-on-one conversation with a friend. They are able to bring their natural selves to their presentations, albeit a prepared and polished version of themselves. If you're inviting people over to your house for dinner, you're likely to do some tidying up, but you don't remodel the whole house. The same is true of speaking. We tidy up and organize our words and have a map, but we still want to speak in our natural voices and be our authentic selves.

Rest assured that if you are thoughtful and subdued in "real life," you can be thoughtful and subdued when speaking. It's just that you'll add delivery skills to help energize and animate to add dynamics to your presentation. If you're a gregarious and energetic person in your everyday exchanges, you should be gregarious and energetic in front of an audience, with a few added delivery skills to help you to appear calm, composed, and credible.

No personality transplant is required to become a skilled speaker.

Good delivery skills eliminate distracting behaviors and help you to use your body, face, and voice in intentional ways to further your message. What people want is your truest, most authentic self, not a slick performance. In fact, if a speaker is too slick listeners can feel disengaged rather than connected to the speaker, and by extension, her ideas.

Here's the problem: Nerves and/or excitement can cause us to do very "unnatural" things in front of an audience. We bite our lips, wring our hands, pace, fidget, mumble, rush, chatter, fuss with our hair or clothing, blink excessively, repeat non-words like *um* and *er*, grimace, furrow our brows, over-smile during serious moments, smack our lips, and display a host of other distracting behaviors. What's weird is that if were we sitting around a table with trusted friends telling the same story, these behaviors wouldn't be there at all, or in such small amounts they'd go unnoticed. These distracting behaviors are symptoms of nerves, excitement, and often self-consciousness. What we want to do in preparation for speaking events is to strip away these symptoms, and add behaviors that are in congruence with the story we're telling.

The simple skills I'll teach here are highly effective at eliminating distracting behaviors, making you feel calmer and more at ease, and helping your natural self to show up at the front of the room, at an interviewer's microphone, or at a table with an agent while you pitch your book idea. In short, these skills help you look more like you—at your best. Before we dig in, one small mental shift.

MENTAL SHIFT

"Simple" and "Easy" are Not Synonyms
The physical skills for speaking with confidence and authenticity are supremely simple. None of them require physical prowess, strength, or a particular body style or athletic ability. The best delivery skills are "simple". They are not, however, "easy".

Changing how we use our face, hands, voice, or body requires practice. Our habits may be small, but they're tricky to change. It can feel frustrating when you try to change something so seemingly simple. Be patient with yourself. Habits that took a long time to create require time and practice to change.

Pros Started as Beginners Too

"All of the great speakers were bad speakers at first."
—Ralph Waldo Emerson

When we measure ourselves and our speaking abilities against the most famous and accomplished speakers of our time and icons in history, we inevitably come up short. It's important to note that those celebrities and icons did not all start out with their abilities. They've practiced. They've learned. Many have received coaching. Very few people pop onto the scene with the speaking abilities that we envy—they learned them.

Many list Oprah Winfrey as a speaker they admire. If she's not your cup of tea, that's okay, but you have to admire what she's accomplished. What's important to know is that Winfrey was told in her early career that she'd never make it in TV. This was long before she hosted the talk show that made her most famous. (She clearly ignored that input.)

Even after she'd begun hosting her show, Winfrey was still honing her skills. I challenge you to do a search and watch the introduction she makes on her very first national show. She is skilled, but she is not the Oprah her listeners expect today. She's clearly excited, and likely quite nervous about her new show. She's jumpy. She talks too fast and barely breathes or pauses. She laughs nervously. She speaks over her guests. Even Oprah started as a beginner.

Make It Stick

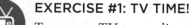 **EXERCISE #1: TV TIME!**
Tune your TV to any live talk show. It'll be more helpful if you can view a couple of different kinds of shows to do this exercise. Select non-scripted shows where people are speaking extemporaneously (not reading a script or a teleprompter): a talk show, a one-on-one interview, or a panel discussion.

Step 1. Turn off the sound and observe the participants. Look closely for the following:

- How much can you infer about the person and her message from just how she's using his body?
- Do you see evidence of nerves? Frustration? Impatience? Amusement?

Step 2: Turn the sound back on to see if what the person is saying matches the body posture you observed.

- Is your impression different with the words?
- Are there contradictions between what the words are saying and what the speaker's body is saying?

Step 3: Keep the sound on, but close your eyes.

- Notice the quality of the voices (not the words being said). What do you hear?

By observing Amy Cuddy's TED Talk referenced earlier and doing the above exercise, you're ready to start digging into the delivery skills.

CHAPTER 13

Control the Climate with Delivery Skills

Delivery skills are a huge part of how you can influence the tone, or what I'm calling the "climate," of your presentations. Whatever your topic and your personality style, finding the right emotional and interactive temperature can serve your topic. Here's how I think of it:

How Do You Want To Be Perceived?

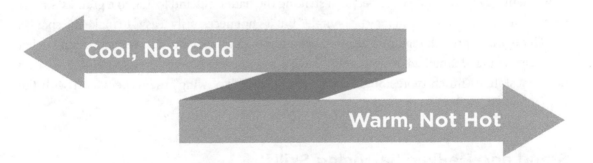

TOO COLD	COOL	WARM	TOO HOT
Icy	Relaxed	Friendly	Jumpy
Aloof	Calm	Animated	Frenetic
Wooden	Credible	Welcoming	Out of control

Every presentation has the same goals, though the style and personality of the presenter and the subject may be wildly different between talks. The universal goals are:

- We want to engage our listeners' senses, emotions, and curiosity.
- We want them to see us as credible presenters on our topics.
- We want listeners to recognize the value of what we're saying.
- We want to appear composed, as though we have plenty of time (even if we don't) to say what we've selected to say, without rushing.
- We want to capture and hold attention.
- We want listeners to be intrigued and to want to know more.
- Sometimes we want listeners to think or behave differently as a result of our talk.
- We want audiences to see us as authentic, natural, believable, and (*usually) likeable.

*There is that rare presenter who seems not to care about being likeable: shock jocks, political provocateurs, and some edgier comedians. They gain popularity with their "unlikeable" style. Most presenters benefit more from a warmer reception and from the quality of being likeable.

The list above is the "what" that we all want. Now let's get specific about "how" to get it. This is where delivery skills kick in. Again, delivery skills are more akin to athletics than they are an intellectual exercise. For an ace baseball pitcher, the smallest adjustment in his pitching movement can be the difference between striking the batter out and losing to a grand slam. As we said earlier, the adjustment may be "simple," but it's not necessarily "easy" to make the change.

Change and growth require, first, our awareness of our behaviors and, second, practice that can help us make small adjustments that have a big impact. It takes practice, and mastering delivery skills is much more about "doing" them than "knowing" them. Let's start with the knowing, and we'll move to the doing.

Stand and Deliver: Balancing Skills

These are the same skills I once taught to a group of funeral directors who had to communicate burial options to the bereaved, and to a sales team at an international sportswear company launching a new line of soccer equipment as well as authors launching books in all kinds of genres. They work for everybody, and you'll find the right temperature that works for you.

What you're seeking in delivery skills is a balance between composure (cool) and energy (warm). But if you tell me to "be composed" or to "be energetic," I still don't know what to do. I'll break it down to the super-simple skills.

COMPOSURE SKILLS

- Stance
- Silence
- Sustained

ENERGY SKILLS

Animation of

- Body
- Face
- Voice

At this point, composure and energy skills likely just seem like vague terms. Let's break them down. The next two chapters will be devoted to these composure and energy skills. I'll break them down and offer lots of examples.

CHAPTER 14

Cool Things Down With Composure Skills

The composure skills (Stance, Silence, and Sustained Eye Contact) do several great big jobs for you:

1. They build your credibility by making you appear calm.
2. They help your listeners relax and take in what you are saying because they have a sense that you know where you're going, and they're willing to trust you to take them there.
3. They help you manage your nervousness and excitement so that you make moves that are intentional, rather than reactive.

Stance

Your body starts speaking before you utter a word. How you position your body, hold your arms, and balance your weight can communicate either in harmony with your message, or compete with it. If you walk into a meeting with a boss and she is standing at the front of the room with her arms crossed in front of her chest and her shoulders scrunched tightly, what is your impression? By the same token, if a speaker is leaning against a table with his hands in his pockets, does this give you the impression he's got big exciting news or an urgent announcement? Perhaps not.

What I seek from a stance is that it says nothing that I do not intend. It's a default posture, which achieves a balance between alert and relaxed. Alert/relaxed is about the impression the stance gives to viewers and the sensation it provides for you, the speaker. As a speaker, you want to appear alert and ready, but not tense or wound too tightly.

Here's the default stance I recommend. I start every talk in this position and return to it many times throughout. This stance does not "accidentally speak" for me, but lets me determine what message I'm delivering with my words and *intentional* body movements. Here's the default stance that I think of as "neutral":

- **Feet about hip-width apart for a steady foundation** (If your feet are too close together, you sway like a flagpole in the wind; too far apart, and you look like a coach on the sidelines.)
- **Weight balanced on both feet** (Avoid rocking, swaying, and shifting your weight from side to side.)
- **Knees loose, not locked** (Tight knees and thighs cut off circulation which can make you feel panicky and nervous.)
- **Hips even** (Again, to avoid rocking.)
- **Shoulders level/chest up** (Think of a thread tugging your chest straight up toward the ceiling. An erect torso increases lung capacity. Breathing is good!)
- **Head vertical** (A tilted head implies a lack of confidence or a question, rather than a statement. It can even come across as unintentionally flirtatious. It's okay to go there intentionally, but not as a habit.)
- **Arms relaxed at your sides, hands relaxed down to the fingertips** (This one will feel strange at first and you will use your hands and arms for animation, but return them to your sides between gestures.)

When we are nervous or unsure, our tendency is to make our bodies smaller. We scrunch our shoulders, cross our legs, or clutch our hands together. All of these make us appear self-conscious, not confident. By extending our bodies to their full height, increasing lung capacity, resisting covering ourselves with our arms, and standing on a firm foundation, we give the impression of confidence. Not only that, adopting this posture can make us *feel* more confident.

I am not recommending that you stand in this neutral position for the whole talk—that would look bizarre. This is the "home base" position, the one you'll begin with, end with, and come back to many times throughout your talk.

Silence

"Silence is also conversation."
—Ramana Marshi, Hindu sage

I have a lot to say about silence. Please indulge me. It's important.

If I had time to teach only two delivery skills to instantly transform every single person into a better public speaker, I'd choose silence and sustained eye contact. Though I list them as composure skills (and they are), they are also powerful in terms of their impact on both the speaker and the audience. I'll spend a bit of time and a few pages on each.

Learning to add (and welcome) silence into your speaking style requires practice and, almost always, listening to yourself in a recording. We tend not to hear how we are, or are not, using silence as we speak. We may be unaware of how quickly we speak, how much we repeat ourselves, or how many non-words (like *um* and *er*) we use.

By adding silence to your talk, you can instantly raise the audience's perception of your level of expertise, credibility, and authority as a speaker.

Most speakers chatter. They're afraid of running out of time—perhaps they've over packed and have too much content—or they're nervous or excited. The big bummer is that chattering lowers the perception of your credibility. Rather than sounding like an authority on a subject, when we chatter we sound more like little girls at a slumber party.

In music, the rests (or the silences) are as important as the notes. Imagine Beethoven's *Fifth Symphony* or Aretha Franklin's "Respect" without those dramatic silences between musical phrases, to say nothing of the melodic and rhythmic variations. Music without rests is not music; it's just a clutter of notes. The same is true when speaking. Speaking without rests isn't storytelling—it's just words.

Silence—pausing between words, phrases, or sentences—serves as the musical "rests" between our spoken words.

"I have spent most of the day putting in a comma and the rest of the day taking it out."
—Oscar Wilde

Writers, you know the value of punctuation and white space on the page. Imagine if you wrote a chapter of a book with no spaces between the words, no tabs for new paragraphs, and no margins at the edges of the page. You may have the best story in the world, but it would be unreadable. Why is that? Why is the white space on the page important?

White space between sentences, paragraphs, scenes, and chapters allows the reader to absorb what has just been written and prepare to transition to the next idea. The same is true of speaking. If we rat-a-tat our words out hurriedly, with no pauses, it's difficult for listeners not only to hear our words, but, more importantly, it becomes difficult for them to "experience" what we're saying.

Many of my clients over the years have been told that they talk too fast. I've learned—through a lot of trial and error—that the rate of one's speech is stubborn to change. It seems to be hardwired because of personality, culture, and the region where the speaker grew up. Most people don't speak too quickly—they simply speak too *continuously*. Pausing allows even the fastest talkers to be heard and understood. While the rate of our speech is difficult to change, anybody can learn to add silence to their speaking.

Don't Talk during My Movie!

Imagine yourself in a movie theater. You've found your seat, you have your popcorn, and you're excited to see the film. Just as the show starts, the couple behind you starts to talk, voicing their every reaction to what's on the screen. Do you love that? Of course not, but why not? It's because they're distracting you from the film. They're talking during *your* movie and breaking the trance the filmmaker is creating for you.

This happens when you're speaking, too. You describe a vivid image to your listeners, a Spellbinder perhaps. What you're asking them to do is conjure that image like a mini-movie in their minds. It takes only a second or two for these mini-movies to form. If you don't pause long enough for listeners to conjure the image, and you continue on with your next idea, *you're breaking the trance*.

Listeners are far more likely to have a connection to what you're saying if they have a chance to have an emotional or intellectual experience of it. That takes place in the brief seconds of silence. If you talk over their internalizing of what you've just said, *you're talking during their movie!*

How Much Silence?

Silence is auditory punctuation. Different punctuation indicates different lengths of pauses between ideas. Periods, commas, dashes, semicolons, line and section breaks are all provided so that your reader can absorb what she just read and prepare for the transition to what's next. At the end of chapters, we often leave lots of white space, sometimes even whole blank pages. The bigger the transition, the larger the white space. The same is true when we're speaking. There are different lengths of silence depending on what you're trying to communicate.

You'll pause briefly between sentences, longer between paragraphs, and longer still as you transition from your Setup to your Itinerary, or from one Chapter of your spoken Story Map to another. The more vivid, important, startling, funny, or complex a stated idea is, the longer your listeners need to absorb it and have an emotional or intellectual experience of it. The bigger the transition to the next idea, the longer the pause should be.

It's during the silence that the real impact of your words will hit your listeners. You need to get out of the way and let them have their own reactions.

A Presentation Full of Weeds

Our lips cannot keep up with our thoughts. That, coupled with our natural discomfort with silence, causes us to talk when we're not yet sure of what we're going to say. The result of that is a lot of non-words or sounds: the "ums" and "ers" of speaking. A "non-word" is any word or sound that does not add any meaning to the sentence.

Some non-words are actual words, but used in a repetitive way or a way that adds no meaning: *like, you know, so, well, basically, actually, okay, right*, and so on. Some entire phrases function as non-words—they're words, but add no meaning to the sentence: "*At the end of the day*," "*When all is said and done*," "*Honestly speaking*," and many more. These are the words in our written work that we edit out.

Some non-words are generational. In the '70s, "man" could have been considered a non-word for its frequency of use. In 2017, the trend words might be "dude" or "yo" for today's younger speakers. While there's nothing wrong with using fun vernacular (particularly if it's an intentional part of a presenter's "voice"), we have choices to make about whether using them frequently (or unconsciously) serves to give the impression we are striving for as a speaker.

It's natural to have a few non-words whenever we speak. That's no big deal. When the non-words become repetitive, or there are too many of them, they become noticeable. Even those people regarded as skilled speakers use some non-words, more in their extemporaneous speaking than in prepared talks.

I think of non-words as weeds. If you have a beautiful garden and you have a few weeds in it, those weeds are unimportant, and often go unnoticed. If you have more weeds than flowers, the garden isn't so pretty.

Weeding Your Word Garden

If non-words are weeds, after years of trying a dozen other methods, I now know the only effective weed killer. It's this: *shorter sentences and longer pauses*. Period. End of story. I've tried dozens of other techniques to help my clients reduce non-words, but this is the only one that works.

Personality, culture, and the region where we grew up largely determine the rate at which we each speak. It's unlikely that any coaching will slow the speech of a fast-talking New Yorker, nor speed up the speech of a Texan. It's baked in. The faster you talk, the more pauses you'll need so that your audience can absorb and envision the story you're telling. The bigger the idea you're conveying, the longer the pause; sometimes even a dramatic Grand Canyon of a pause is warranted when you want your listeners to deeply absorb an idea or an image.

By shortening sentences and adding silence (like white space on a page) you'll eliminate most non-words.

Why is it important to eliminate excessive non-words? They dilute our intended words and messages. *I'm, like, y'know, um, sorry,* just doesn't have the same impact as the uncluttered *I'm sorry.*

Silence Serves Multicultural Audiences

If you're speaking in your second language, you'll likely use more non-words. Pausing will help with that because, in the silence, you're able to conjure and translate the words you're searching for. If you speak with an accent, pauses will let your listeners decipher your inflection and pronunciation. If you're speaking to a multicultural audience who might be listening in *their* second languages, silence will allow them to hear, translate, and interpret your words.

Without silence in which multi-cultural speakers and listeners can do their quick mental translations, much is literally lost in translation.

Silence Is the Best Medicine for Nerves

"If we're growing, we're always going out of our comfort zone."
—John C. Maxwell, author/pastor

The most nervous speakers I've ever seen (and this includes myself) bring two types of anxiety to the experience:

1. **Psychological anxiety** (worry, fear, self-consciousness, and so on).
2. **Physiological (physical) anxiety** that they create (unintentionally) in their bodies, right in front of their audience.

A big portion of physical anxiety comes from a lack of oxygen. It's a vicious cycle.

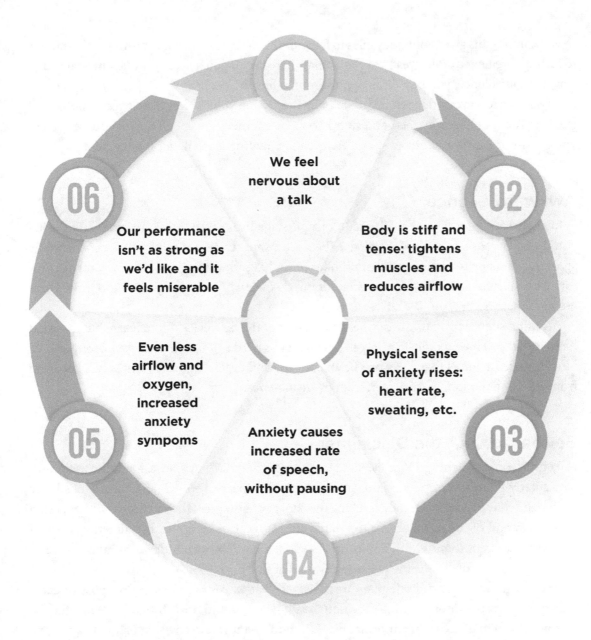

01 We feel nervous about a talk

02 Body is stiff and tense: tightens muscles and reduces airflow

03 Physical sense of anxiety rises: heart rate, sweating, etc.

04 Anxiety causes increased rate of speech, without pausing

05 Even less airflow and oxygen, increased anxiety sympoms

06 Our performance isn't as strong as we'd like and it feels miserable

When you don't pause and you don't breathe deeply, your body and mind fill with a mix of anxiety soup. A deceptively simple remedy for in-the-moment anxiety while speaking is this: *pause, relax your muscles, and breathe.*

It sounds so simple. It's harder to do.

When we're tense, we stand with our knees cocked and thigh muscles tightened, shoulders crunched, and we breathe shallowly. Standing this way constricts blood flow and limits oxygen to your brain. This gives your body cues to fight, fright, or freeze—our most primitive responses to feeling threatened. You sweat. Your heart rate increases. If you deliver your talk in a rapid-fire way, without silence, you have little opportunity to breathe deeply.

Use silence as your opportunity to breathe deeply. Sip your water. Check your notes. *Oxygenate.* (Turns out breathing is good stuff.) You'll be stunned how much this will serve to calm you and improve your ability to speak. Rather than inviting fear, silence invites calm.

Awkward Silence

While we encounter awkward silence in our off-stage lives all the time—particularly during emotional encounters—awkward silence (because a speaker pauses too long) is rare in public speaking. Pausing too long is a risk most of us never have to worry about. Our natural discomfort with silence generally keeps us from doing this. Nearly everyone pauses too little. Odds are high that you do, too.

Adding silence by pausing may be the toughest of the delivery skills to learn, but the good news is that you have a built-in safety net. If you try as hard as you can to pause uncomfortably long, my prediction is that you won't be able to. Your natural self-consciousness will keep you from standing too long in silence in front of an audience.

Be the Ad, Not the Disclaimer

Next time you're watching TV or listening to commercial radio, pay special attention to the ads, particularly pharmaceutical ads and car ads. Notice the pace of speech and the use of silence during the commercial while they're telling the "story" of how great their product is. Then, listen to the very end of the commercial. That rapid-fire delivery of all of the disclaimers at the end feels very different than the ad, doesn't it? It's spoken quickly, with little voice inflection, and with no pauses at all. This is the verbal equivalent of fine print.

Fine print and verbal disclaimers are delivered that way for the express purpose of camouflaging negative information—they don't really want you to absorb that part, but they're legally obliged to disclose that information. They don't want you to envision balloon payments, limited warranties, or side effects that could include cancer, excessive bleeding, or death. The disclaimer is the ultimate "talking during your movie" before you even get a chance to envision it. And it's intentional.

Ask yourself this: Do you want to sound like the ad or the disclaimer when you talk about your book, your projects, or your ideas? The difference is silence.

One Last Pitch for Silence

The irony is not lost on me that I use a great many words to laud the value of silence. That's okay, it's really important so I'm willing to live with the contradiction.

Lots of my coaching clients have voiced concerns that if they pause as much as I suggest, they won't have enough time to cover all of their material. I give you a choice: Would you prefer to say fewer things while making a memorable connection with your listeners, or more things and have them disengaged from you and the story you're telling? The answer is obvious. It's infinitely better to say fewer things with impact than more things without it. It's during the pauses that your listeners experience the emotional, intellectual, and psychological impact of what you're saying.

There's another reason that using silence doesn't rob you of speaking time. Time for a quick mental shift.

MENTAL SHIFT

Pausing may add no time at all.

Silence, when used to eliminate non-words, requires no extra time. It's just that your listeners hear calm silence rather than a clutter of nonsense syllables. During the silence, your audience absorbs what you've said, and you think of the precise word you want to use.

Sentence one: *I'm going to the um store to get, y'know, um butter, and um, eggs, and-ah milk. Because, y'know, um, I'm like, going to make, y'know a cake*

Sentence two: I'm going to the (short silence) store to get, (silence) butter, (silence), and eggs. (Longer silence). I'm going to make a cake.

It's when we rush that we add the "weeds" into our speaking.

Speak *Only* to People

"Eye contact: how souls catch fire."
—Yahia Lababidi, poet

I offer guidelines and coaching and suggestions throughout this book, but have only one *unbreakable* rule about delivery skills and it's this: ***You are only allowed to speak to people.*** That means that when you're the speaker, you must be looking at a person in order to speak. If you need to check your notes, navigate your computer screen, or write on a whiteboard, you must, as my very Southern aunt once told all of us kids, *shut your pie hole, darlin's*. Use silence to help you focus on other tasks like checking your notes. If you try to talk while you're doing something other than focusing on a listener, you'll appear distracted—because you are.

If you talk while not connected to a person's eyes, you run the risk of looking aloof and disengaged from your listeners. Speakers often mumble into the carpet or talk while they're gathering their thoughts, looking up at the ceiling. Use silence when you're thinking, checking notes, or navigating technology. It lets your listeners reflect and it allows you to focus on your task and get it done quickly and efficiently.

You know that feeling when you're at a mixer and you're talking with someone who is looking around the room while she speaks or listens to you? The feeling I get in this situation is that there's someone else she'd rather be speaking with. This is the feeling your audience members will have if you're talking to them while doing something else. You give the impression that your task is more important than your listeners. Focused, sustained eye contact is the single biggest connection tool you have.

The fabulous singer Marilyn Maye was interviewed by the one-of-a-kind Mo Rocca on the CBS *Sunday Morning* show. In it, Rocca makes an unusual observation to a singer: "You're not shy about making eye contact." To which Maye replied, "Oh no. That's the whole purpose. It's to tell you the story of the song." In his commentary about the piece, Rocca states, "For many, the secret to connecting to an audience comes down to a simple preposition: singing *to* them, not *for* them."

Though Rocca is talking about singers, this is equally true for speakers. Lots of speakers think they're sustaining eye contact, when actually they're scanning the room or their eyes are darting from place to place.

Here's how I think of it: Think of each person in the room as a potted plant. I know . . . stay with me on this. Think of your eye contact as the water coming from a watering can. You don't want to just spray the whole room, you want to water each plant, one by one, letting the water soak in, down to the roots of the plant. How much water/eye contact should you give? The answer is, you don't want a fleeting glance with each person, you want a meaningful connection.

Here are the guidelines I offer for sustained eye contact in a group of five or more:

- **In Western cultures, eye contact with each person when you're in a group should be about three to six seconds in length.** This is long enough to complete two very short, or one medium-length sentence with a person before switching to another.
- **In Eastern cultures, eye contact is generally shorter than in Western cultures.** Too long and eye contact can be experienced as aggressive or rude by some cultures.
- **Avoid a predictable pattern with your eye contact.** Eye contact should be randomly distributed. Imagine telling a story at a large dinner party with friends. Your eyes would pop randomly to each guest, in no particular pattern. The same is true

when speaking in public—you just have a bigger table and more friends to include. The key here is random eye contact in an unpredictable pattern.

- **Avoid darting back and forth, ping-pong style with your eyes.** This gives the impression of nervousness or dishonesty, even if you're telling the truth. Think of the expression "shifty-eyed." It means sneaky—the last impression you want to give to your listeners.

- **Share the love and leave no orphans.** Don't just make eye contact with the smiling, friendly faces in the room. Some people wear grumpy or sleepy looks when they're listening. Include them as well. If you're co-presenting or on a panel, include your colleagues in your eye contact. No presentation orphans—everybody is invited to the party!

- **If you need an extended silence to think, check your notes, or fix a technology problem, break eye contact.** Doing so helps you focus. If it's a brief tech problem fixed in a few seconds, you needn't acknowledge it. If the problem requires longer, excuse yourself from your listeners for a moment, tend to the issue, and return to eye contact to move forward with or without your tech functioning.

- **Use eye contact to read your listeners' mood, comfort level, and engagement level with you and your material. Eye contact is a two-way communication.** If you observe a lot of furrowed brows or fidgets, adjust your pace, introduce interaction to re-engage your listeners, or ask for questions.

- **In very large groups, use the same technique, with one tweak:** If you're speaking in a large forum with fifty, a hundred, or a thousand people (it could happen), you can't keep track of every pair of eyes and how long you're speaking to each person. Nonetheless, employ the same techniques as described above. Distribute your sustained eye contact to every corner of the room. Find a face, and linger for three to six seconds. Those seated farthest from you cannot tell exactly where your eyes are fixed. Those around the person you're looking at will "inherit" eye contact and feel included. (I call this the rock star effect. Everyone leaves the concert feeling like their idol looked right at them.)

- **Follow your listener's cues:** I'm often asked how a speaker would know if they're lingering in eye contact for too long. Individuals have different preferences when it comes to eye contact. If you're looking at someone, and you linger in their eyes for longer than they're comfortable, they'll look away. No need to "eye stalk" them and insist on more than they want. We naturally make these adjustments all the time in our everyday lives without even being conscious of doing so. Trust yourself. You won't stare someone down. Chances are much higher that your eye contact in a large group is too fleeting.

Sustained Eye Contact Shrinks the Audience

"You think Superman could talk to a thousand people? He could get their attention, but he has to bend something first. But to just get up . . . and start talking?"
—Chris Rock, comedian

To this day, I never do "public speaking" events. Oh, I speak in front of people all of the time, sometimes to large groups of people. It's just that I don't' speak to all of them at once. That's too intimidating for this recovering glossophobe. Rather than talking to "an audience", I prefer to think that I'm having a series of one-on-one conversations with however many people are in the room.

> ## MENTAL SHIFT
>
> **If you try to talk to everybody, you're really connecting to nobody.**
> Make it intimate, connected, and natural with sustained eye contact with one person at a time. Lots of speakers try to talk to the whole group at once. Their eyes scan and dart. They can appear freaked out.

"Never make eye contact while eating a banana."
—Unknown

There are times when you should not sustain eye contact. When you are neither talking nor listening to someone speaking to you, it's awkward to sustain eye contact with an audience member. Standing silently or walking toward a participant silently while sustaining eye contact can come off rather creepy. If you need to think for a bit, consider an idea, or generally be quiet so you can determine your next phrase, break eye contact and be quiet. If you're speaking and you choose to walk around the room a bit (as I'll describe in energy skills), don't walk silently while your eyes are fixed on an audience member. It'll make them feel as though they need to obtain a restraining order! (Just kidding. But you get the point.)

Stance, Silence, and Sustained Eye Contact enable you, the speaker, to feel calmer, to gather your thoughts, to breathe, and to connect to your listeners. These three skills combined add up to composure. They'll help you manage nerves, lower your heart rate, and at first appear, then literally become, calmer in front of a group of listeners.

In our next chapter, we'll add dynamics to the delivery skills by adding energy skills to the mix. But first, let's get these composure skills down in your bones.

Make It Stick

EXERCISE #1: LEARN FROM A SINGER AS STORYTELLER
Search YouTube for Marilyn Maye, CBS *Sunday Morning*. Watch her interview and her performance. She has been on the stage for seventy years, and you'll soon see why. Watch particularly for how she uses eye contact with her audience, how natural and spontaneous she is with her listeners, and the impact this has on her sung version of storytelling. Learn from a master!

EXERCISE #2: FUN HOMEWORK
Newscasters and comedians are among the most skilled at using silence effectively. I invite you to take special notice of these two types of presentation.

1. Tune into Your National Evening News. Observe the news anchor. Of course, she's reading off of a teleprompter, so she'll use very few, if any, non-words. I'd like you to observe how she uses pause for emphasis, punctuation, and dramatic effect. You'll notice, if you watch a panel or interview show, that speakers use fewer pauses (often they're competing for air space) and that non-words creep back in.

2. Watch the Sports and News Reporters. Observe how their delivery skills differ from the news anchor's style. What impact do the two styles have?

3: Watch Your Favorite Comedian. Tune in either online, on your TV, or better yet, at a local live performance. You can even listen to comedy albums. Call it homework. *You're welcome.* Pay attention to the comedian's use of silence. She tells the beginning of a joke, pauses . . . lets you imagine a possible punch line . . . pauses again. Then she delivers the punch line (likely a different one than the one you imagined) and does what? Right, she uses silence again while you get the joke. Silence allows his audience to get the joke and makes room for the laugh.

EXERCISE #3: NOTICE THE EFFECT OF SILENCE IN SPEAKING.
Combined with sustained eye contact, silence is what gives the appearance of composure. The only way to learn to infuse silence into your speech is to try it for yourself. I offer a simple exercise.

- Use your smart phone or another recording device. Without worrying about the quality of the content (it doesn't matter here) talk for one to three minutes about the following: Tell the story of your first job. Describe it. How did you get it? Did you like it? How much did it pay? What was your boss like? Don't worry if you don't finish the story.
- Listen back. See which non-words you tended to use. Make note. What are they? How many of them did you use?
- Then tell the same story again. This time, pause between every sentence. Pause longer between what would be paragraphs. Your speech will feel stilted and a little boring. That's okay, it's just to learn the skill of using silence. You can add the fun back in later.
- Listen back. Note the non-words. Are there fewer? Different ones?

CHAPTER 15

Warm Up Your Talk with Energy Skills

I addressed composure first in the prior chapter because It's a good foundation to build upon in terms of delivery skills. Composure skills alone will get you far. They'll help you feel calmer, give your audience the impression that you're a trustworthy tour guide to the story journey on which you'll take them, and it helps you to stay on course with your content. Most importantly, those composure skills invite your audience into the story you're telling, whether they interact silently or verbally.

While the composure skills are essential, if you practice them alone a talk could come off as flat, lifeless, and (yikes) boring. You could be perceived as detached, disinterested, and without passion for your topic. This is where adding energy skills can change everything.

Once you've figured out how to look and feel composed in front of a group, it's easier to add energy. If composure is about stillness and silence, energy is about sound and movement.

The name of the game in energy skills is "animation." The skills are body animation, facial animation, and vocal animation. Let's take them one at a time.

Body Animation: Movement

"Stop acting so small. You are the universe in ecstatic motion."
—Rumi

I often have to coach my speaking clients to "take up some room." You do this with your body, with your voice, and with your energy. The stage is yours when you're the speaker. This doesn't mean that you are garish or inappropriate, or dominating and intimidating your listeners. It's just that by literally and energetically taking up room, you convey confidence. One of the best ways to take up room is to animate yourself.

There are two ways to animate your body; one is to move it around the room, and the other is to use hand and body gestures.

Let's look first at **movement.** Many venues don't lend themselves to moving around as you talk. Bookstores, for example, usually have a lectern and a microphone, which will keep you pretty well fixed in one spot which lends itself to reading. It's the same with many keynote addresses and other "stage" kind of events. That's okay. But when a venue or the event lends itself to it, I find that movement helps both the audience and the presenter stay energized and engaged. It gives the audience visual variety and it helps the presenter manage (or revive) her energy, as well as do a little subtle and sophisticated behavior management of the group.

Have you noticed if you're standing in line for a long time how tired your legs get? To "rest" from a long bit of standing, we have the urge to walk it off. The same is true when speaking. For a short talk at a lectern, standing isn't tiring or boring. But if you were to deliver a three-hour workshop, standing in one place would be not only exhausting for you; it would be tedious for your listeners. Making use of the space, walking around to connect to listeners, and providing a little variety adds energy to your talk.

Changing your location can also help you manage participant interaction. By positioning yourself close to a couple of Chatty Cathys who are distracting to the group, you can encourage them to quiet down without making them feel scolded. By stepping casually toward a quiet participant while making eye contact, you can invite her to participate simply by your proximity.

When you move, don't mosey. Move with intention and in the direction of your toes. (Walking backward or side-stepping is a recipe for disaster.)

Here's the important thing to remember about movement: *Move when you're moving, stand still when you're standing still.*

Most people *think* they're standing still but they're rocking, fidgeting, or twitching. This is moving while standing still and it gives the impression of nervousness. Other people *think* they're moving, but their steps are halting—think Frankenstein's monster taking one plodding step at a time. Speakers think they're moving, but if it's not powerful, intentional movement, rather than add energy, it stops it.

Move (with intention) when you're moving, stand still (calmly and without fidgeting) when you're standing still.

If you do walk around the room, come to rest occasionally rather than walking continuously. Walking without stopping looks like frantic pacing, not powerful movement. Come to rest and resume that calm, steady stance between movements.

Go anywhere in the room that the geography allows and avoid a back-and-forth pacing pattern. Surprise your listeners. I often challenge speakers whom I coach with what I call The Star Trek Challenge. "Go where no man has gone before."

Body Animation: Gestures

The second part of body animation is the use of **gestures.**

In poker there's a concept called the "tell." This is where a player gives away what's in her hand by some unintentional facial expression or gesture. His body "tells" the other players when he's bluffing or holding a fist full of aces.

For speakers, the "tell" often arrives as a gesture. Twitching fingers reveal our nerves. Clasped hands show our hesitation. Fussing with hair or clothing makes our self-consciousness more apparent. A clenched fist or crossed arms belies our frustration or defensiveness.

There are times in a public presentation when you want to play some cards close to the vest— like if you're nervous, if you've lost your place in your talk, or if you forgot to say something that you'd intended in the prior section. Hiding these cards doesn't mean you are inauthentic, just that you are choosing to lead with your confidence rather than your hesitation.

What's the purpose of using gestures anyway? If you've ever given directions while talking on the phone and caught yourself gesturing the turns and forming the landmarks with your free hand, you know that gestures are not just for the listener. Gestures help the speaker track her thoughts. What you're doing when you gesture is animating your thoughts and words into a visual. This helps listeners to pay attention, to "see" what you're saying. Gestures also help you to track your thinking. Win, win.

To transform your gestures from distracting to intentional, here are a few guidelines:

1. **Gestures should be bigger than you think and higher than you think.** Often you'll see speakers fiddling with their fingers, or gesturing from the wrists, in front of their tummies. Instead, gestures should be from the shoulder, should frame your face (rather than your bellybutton), and can use your entire wingspan. It may feel extreme, but it looks more natural than fluttery gestures. Just watch when a friend is describing an exciting sports event or a funny scene and you'll see how big natural gestures actually are.

2. **Avoid gestures that get "stuck."** These include clasping your hands in front of your body, folding your arms, tucking your hands into pockets, or locking them behind your back. All of these gestures may feel comfortable to you as the presenter by making you feel sheltered behind a little wall you create. Such shielding gestures

may feel good, but communicate a lack of confidence, defensiveness, or, in the case of hands in the pockets, sloppiness or apathy. If you intentionally use a gesture like these now and then for effect, that's fine, but be cautious. Once your hands find one another, you can drift into that comfort zone and get stuck in that position. Your words may say one thing, but your body will contradict it. If you let your arms drop to your sides and "dangle" (not tense) there between gestures, you'll appear open, relaxed, and unguarded.

3. **Use a variety of gestures.** If you watch the same speaker for any length of time, you'll start to recognize their go-to gestures. Impersonators make a lot of hay when they pick up a politician's or celebrity's go-to gestures because it makes them easier to imitate. Try varying your gestures. Use just one hand now and then, instead of making every gesture a mirror image between the hands. Make some vertical, some horizontal, some close to the body, some to imply motion. Anything you do over and over again in front of an audience becomes annoying, boring, distracting, or all three. Change it up!

4. **"Let" gestures match your content and emotional proportion.** Rather than telling you how to move your arms, I'd rather tell you to "let" yourself gesture. Gesturing is natural and organic. If you're among friends, telling an animated story, I'll bet you gesture without thinking about what gesture to make. I'd also bet that you gesture bigger and more animatedly than you're aware. When speaking in public, I invite you to allow your natural gesturing self to shine.

5. **Give it a rest!** Just as silence is an important part of speaking, stillness is an important part of your delivery skills. Make a gesture from the shoulders, with intention, but then let your arms come to rest. Just as one shouldn't talk continuously without pausing, one should not gesture continuously without coming to rest. Between gestures, return to that neutral Stance. Let your arms fall to your sides, relaxed all the way down to the fingertips. Then make another intentional gesture when your content warrants it.

Notice here that I'm saying "let" your arms fall not "make" your arms fall. Your arms should not be tense or stiff, but relaxed.

Gestures add color to your content. No matter what presentation software you might use, you are the very best visual in the room. Using bigger gestures in wide variety can add a dynamic interest to your talk.

When we are unsure or lack confidence, it is our tendency to make ourselves smaller. We cross our legs, fold our arms, tighten our shoulders up near our ears. All of these body positions clamp off blood flow and create an internal sensation of anxiety. If you're getting less oxygen, your heart beats faster, you perspire more, and breathe more shallowly. By animating your body, you oxygenate your brain, think more clearly, and look and feel more relaxed. Moving and gesturing will go a long way to helping you manage your nerves.

Facial Animation: Match Your Face to Your Content

"People say I look so happy, and I say, 'That's the Botox.'"
—Dolly Parton

When nervous or concentrating, our faces can get into a fixed position—a stiff or scowling face or a false, nervous smile. That fixed resting face can be off-putting and can communicate something we don't intend. We can appear angry or disapproving because we're wearing a "concentrating" face, or we might over-smile out of nervousness, even when we are delivering serious material. Contradiction between our facial expressions and content we are delivering plants seeds of doubt, confusion, or mistrust in the minds of our listeners.

When there's a contradiction between what a person says and the expression she's wearing, we tend to believe what we see rather than what we hear. Of course, this doesn't always split along traditional gender lines, but women tend to over-smile when they're nervous, and men tend to look stern when they're thinking.

Here are a few guidelines for adding facial animation into your presentation tool kit.

1. Wear the face that matches your content in the moment, not what you're anticipating is up next.
2. Find a "pleasant neutral" expression to wear when listening to others or fielding questions. Experiment in the mirror to see if the expression you're feeling is the same as it looks to others.
3. If you know you tend to look serious and smiling is not your natural expression, try lifting your eyebrows to show interest and positive response.
4. Ask for, and welcome, feedback about your facial expressions from a trusted friend or a practice partner prior to an important presentation. Facial animation is in the eye of the beholder.

A huge disparity exists when it comes to our sensations of facial animation. Those who are more introverted or self-conscious feel as though they're expressions are extreme, when often they're barely moving their faces. More extroverted folks feel as though they're barely moving when they're actually overwhelming their listeners with extreme facial expressions. Once again, record yourself. Get feedback. Practice. Whatever your style, it's good to know if you should modify it a bit, and in which direction, in order to have the desired effect on listeners.

Vocal Animation: Use Musical Inspiration to Animate Your Storytelling Voice

Whether you're reading or speaking without a script, your voice is your musical instrument. Music varies from high pitch to low, fast to slow, loud to soft, smooth to rhythmic, and the silences (the rests) have as much impact as the notes. All of these variables should be present in your speaking voice.

People often fear that they sound "monotone" when they speak. More often, rather than being monotone, speakers utilize a limited range of their voice. Here's some good news in the form of a mental shift.

MENTAL SHIFT

If you know how to read to small kids or call to a dog, you know how to animate your voice.
It may seem odd, but the same techniques that you use when attempting to engage with small kids and dogs are the same techniques you'll use to engage a listening audience.

Think of how you'd read a story to a child. You speed up during the active parts of the story and slow down during the thoughtful parts. You pause to create suspense when there is something scary or surprising on the horizon. You change the quality of your voice when reading the villain's dialogue. You whisper during the sneaky parts. But for the silly voices and barnyard animal sounds we might use to bring children's book characters to life, these are the exact techniques to use when you're telling a story to a group of people or when you're reading an excerpt of your own work. Make it suspenseful, scary, moving, funny, or thoughtful—all by using the variety of vocal options you have available.

A few extra hints about animating your voice:

1. **Experiment with rhythm.** For instance, if you're talking along, you can take a pause then punch One. Word. At. A. Time. You'll witness your audience "prairie dogging." Staccato speech is the equivalent of bullet points in writing. You won't use it in every paragraph, but now and then, for emphasis, rhythm change is a great tool. Create variety in rhythm to maintain audience interest.

2. **Change the volume.** Speakers tend to talk at the same volume throughout their talks. Try *raising* your voice to show excitement, frustration, or anger if that's what you're conveying. I don't suggest shouting in most circumstances, but increasing your volume for emphasis can have a big impact. You can whisper when you're implying something special, or letting your audience in on a secret. Whispering draws people in and provides contrast.

3. **Come to a full stop.** An occasional long, dramatic pause is part of your vocal animation package as well as being a composure skill. I try to put a couple of "Grand Canyon" pauses into every talk. This has great impact when you're sharing a poignant, dramatic, surprising, or funny moment.

4. **Just as with facial expressions, your voice should always match your content.** If a loved one or coworker has ever told you that you look or sound angry when you're not, or didn't catch your frustration because you "didn't look angry", this is a clue that your expressions might not always match your content. Time to experiment with a mirror or a recording device so that you can see the disparity between how you "feel" you're appearing or sounding and how you actually come across. Whether conveying happiness, excitement, frustration, or passion, your face should match what you're saying. You can't always assess this from the inside.

But What If I Hate My Voice?

"Sometimes you're a person with a shrill voice and there's nothing you can do about it 'cuz you don't get to choose your voice . . . It was never like, uh 'You know what" I'll take the voice that causes dogs to gather outside'."
—Michelle Wolf, comedian

Clients and workshop participants often say to me, "I just hate my voice." They talk of how shocking it is to hear themselves on recordings, how their voices are annoying, or boring, or sound like their mothers' or fathers' voices. What's interesting is that people with perfectly pleasing voices express the same concerns as those with voices that may be less so.

Voices come in lots of varieties: reedy, shrill, muffled, soothing, mellifluous. Some have accents, lisps, even stutters.

Your voice is your voice, but there's good news. Whatever the quality of your voice, you can embellish it and develop it so that it serves you better. You can take advantage of your voice, no matter its quality. If it's a voice that others might call unusual or peculiar, play it to your advantage. A unique voice—even if you'd prefer to have one of another kind—can be a way to stand out.

David Sedaris, author of *Me Talk Pretty One Day*, is a bestselling author who has traveled the world speaking and promoting his books. He has spoken often about his disdain for the sound of his own voice. His "funny voice" has even been written about in the *New York Times*! Sedaris' voice is high and nasal and he has a slight lisp. What's interesting about this is that Sedaris has made a fortune off of his voice and is a much in-demand speaker. He even narrated the audiobook versions of his books. The mechanics of his voice box are unchangeable, but he makes great use of what he has.

And so can you.

My Personal Note for Poets: Avoid "Weird Poetry Voice"

I love hearing poetry performed more than I enjoy reading it. Unfortunately, a fair number of poets I hear delivering their work at poetry slams and readings articulate their work with such an extreme affect to their voices that it makes me feel squeamish. I love that the voice of a poet becomes her musical instrument and part of her style, and she hones it to suit the genre of her poetry. Sometimes this is great, but sometimes it drifts into another realm.

Too many poets—in my opinion—don a strange character voice (somewhere between a corny beatnik and a Bob Dylan impersonator) when they read or recite their poetry. I called it "weird poet voice" and it turned me off poetry for years. It seems like an affect more than a genuine voice, with an unnatural lilt that not only seems false, but distracts from the poetry itself. While there's a certain "performance" quality to reciting poetry, it should still sound like you, your voice, reading your words, and not as though some stranger has inhabited your voice.

Poets, you have a huge advantage when reading your own work. You know the importance of each word and image. I invite you to use a more natural speaking voice, applying all of the musical elements described above, to interpret your poetry. It will make it much more accessible.

It's fine to have an individual style for delivering your poetry. One poet/philosopher I admire is David Whyte. He has a unique verbal/vocal tool that he uses when he recites his poems. He circles around, repeating phrases multiple times, weaving them in again and again for emphasis. Not everyone can pull this off, but it's a fascinating delivery style and worth listening to if only to illustrate how personal and experimental we can be with our voices. I urge everyone to search for David Whyte clips of all kinds. He's masterful. His audiobooks are fabulous as well. I'm particularly fond of his the audiobook version of his collection, *The Poetry of Self Compassion*.

My Personal Note to Women Writers and Speakers

While the delivery skills shared in part 3 are equally applicable to anyone of any gender or gender identification, I feel compelled to say a special something to women who want to be dynamic, influential speakers.

Published books written by women are a fraction of what is published by male authors, despite the fact that women buy far more books. We can attribute this somewhat to archaic systems in traditional publishing that favor male authors—some of which are changing, others not so much. But ladies, we also need to look at ourselves in this equation and address the attitudes and behaviors that we exhibit that may be getting in our way.

It's been my observation that far too many women as speakers tend to self-deprecate too much, physically make themselves smaller and more diminutive, over-smile when they're sharing troubling news so that it's hard to take their messages seriously, and tend to make their voices extra-high (think "little girl" voice) when they're nervous or intimidated. We tip our heads when we speak, making our statements appear like questions rather than adopting a strong physical stance as I describe it. We are self-conscious about our bodies and tug on our clothing when we speak. We lower our voices so they're hard to hear. We over-apologize for the slightest of errors. We fail to ask boldly for what we want of our listeners. This is true of some of the most talented, powerful, awesome women I know. If this is true in my workshops, I'm guessing it's true during pitches to agents and publishers and at book events as well.

I invite women reading this book to take special note of the physical behaviors (as well as content choices) that diminish our strong image, that make us smaller, and that make us more "girly" and less "womanly," more tentative and less sure. It's part of my personal mission in life to be a champion of the voices of artists, including those of women artists and authors. I invite you to seek and welcome feedback and coaching that helps you to demonstrate the strong, powerful messages and the confidence to which your credentials entitle you. Take up some space. Be bold with your body, your face, your voice *and* your words. Tell your dynamic, fascinating stories. The world needs them.

Animation Gives Spellbinders Superpower

We've already explored the power of Spellbinders, those storytelling tools that make a moment memorable. When you add animation (body, face, hands, and voice) to a Spellbinder, its magical quality expands.

I'd like you to think of movies you've loved, but more than that, of lines from movies you've loved or found memorable. Here are a few famous ones:

- "Here's looking at you, kid." (Humphrey Bogart in *Casablanca*)
- "Fasten your seatbelts. It's going to be a bumpy night." (Bette Davis in *All About Eve*)
- "You're going to need a bigger boat." (Roy Schneider in *Jaws*)
- "Are you crying? There's no crying in baseball!" (Tom Hanks, in *A League of Their Own*)
- "I'll have what she's having." (Estelle Reiner, in *When Harry Met Sally*)

These memorable lines are simple words made memorable because of how they were delivered. The actors *animated* these lines with their faces, voices, and bodies. They used silence to make them stand out.

Make It Stick

EXERCISE #1: DO YOUR DELIVERY SKILLS INVENTORY

Here I invite you to get honest with yourself—really honest—about both your delivery skills strengths and what you might already know are your challenges. Ask yourself the following questions:

1. Do you believe you tend to have more strength in the composure category of delivery skills or in the energy category?
2. What feedback have you been given about your delivery skills? Perhaps from colleagues, loved ones, or audience members? What are the positive comments? What negative comments have you received?
3. Which of the delivery skills described in this chapter seems like the biggest challenge for you? What might you do to practice it and overcome the challenge?
4. What would you guess is your habitual non-word (um, er, like, y'know, okay, right, and others.) If you don't have a clue, ask a coworker or loved one. They'll know.
5. What low-stakes practice opportunities will you seek to help build your delivery skills? Some suggestions: Join Toastmasters. Video or audio record yourself practicing and make note of both strengths and challenges. Seek professional coaching or classes. Experiment with vocal dynamics while reading books to kids. (Dogs like them, too.) Take an improv comedy class to gain confidence and get feedback.

EXERCISE #2: DAVID SEDARIS, READING

I invite you to listen to Sedaris in this YouTube clip as he reads his story "The Incomplete Quad." Notice how he makes use of the "musical" elements of vocal animation as he reads one of his stories. Notice how he uses rhythm, vocal tone, volume, and pause, especially after saying something funny. The story is about twenty minutes long, but worth the listen. Enjoy! (As with all humor, Sedaris's edgy stories are a matter of taste. Whether or not he's your particular flavor of ice cream, I invite you to observe him for the skills he demonstrates with the voice that he was given.)

EXERCISE #3: DAVID WHYTE, "THE JOURNEY"

Do a YouTube search for David Whyte reading his poem "The Journey." It is only a bit over a minute long. Notice how the timbre and style of his speaking voice, prior to starting the poem, doesn't change when his recitation starts. Notice the way that he uses repetition, rhythm, and silence for emphasis.

EXERCISE #4A AND #4B: ELIZABETH GILBERT, TED TALK AND PODCAST

Elizabeth Gilbert has become something of a guru to writers, particularly memoirists, after her phenomenal bestseller *Eat, Pray, Love* in 2006. She gave her TED Talk on "genius" in 2009. Give yourself a present, and let yourself watch this one. The content is terrific, but I'd also like you to observe her delivery skills.

Gilbert is one of the few TED Talkers who clearly delivers her talk in a more conversational way, rather than as a memorized "perfected" talk (though I'm sure it was well rehearsed). I invite you to watch it to notice Gilbert's delivery skills. She has some great ones, but this is not a flawless talk. That's not a criticism. I LOVE that it's not flawless and believe that this is Gilbert's intention. Her entire persona is about being her natural self, flaws and all. Some of the flaws in her initial TED Talk might be due to nerves. She does speak quickly and would benefit from some pausing to eliminate non-words. And still, it's an inspiring talk. Her talk is personal, warm, and heartfelt. After you've watched the talk, ask yourself:

1. What delivery skills (Stance, Sustained eye contact, Silence/Animation of face, voice, and body) does Gilbert use most effectively?
2. What skills could still use some polish?
3. What is the evidence of her nervousness? (Again, no criticism. Who wouldn't be nervous?)

After you've watched Gilbert's TED Talk, I invite you to check out her podcast, "Magic Lessons." She interviews writers and teachers and lots of inspiring people on her podcast, so I'm sure you'll enjoy the content. I'd also like you to notice Gilbert's delivery skills during her podcast. Of course, you can't see her, so the delivery skills you'll note are all audio. Observe:

1. What do you notice about her use of animation as well as silence?
2. What's your impression of the difference between her delivery during her TED Talk and her podcast?

I predict you'll see the growth that Gilbert has made, how much more comfortable she is speaking in a less formal environment, and the poise and confidence she's gained as a speaker.

CHAPTER 16

Delivery Skills Extras and Special Circumstances

The delivery skills—both composure and energy skills—shared in the prior chapters are a great foundation for most any kind of public presentation, be it a prepared talk, a casual exchange, an interview, an agent pitch, or participating on a panel. They're even useful in our personal lives. Couples and families in my therapy practice find it useful to experiment with the tones of their voices and their use of silence in order to communicate better with one another.

A few adaptations to delivery skills are necessary for special circumstances such as those described below. Here are a few extra tools for your public speaking toolbox.

Using a Microphone

Lots of my clients voice hesitancy about using a microphone. A microphone feels conspicuous to them, and seems more like a "performance" device than a "talking" device. At first it feels strange to use a mike and to hear your voice amplified, but it's worth getting used to for the sake of your audience being able to hear you.

My first choice when available is a cordless lavaliere microphone. That's the kind that's pinned onto a collar or lapel and has a small battery pack that you tuck into a pocket. I like not having to worry about tripping on a cord if I choose to move around. I dislike occupying one of my hands by holding a mike, thus inhibiting gestures. A couple of tips for using lavaliere mikes:

- Wear something with a lapel or a place to hook the mike onto at about six inches below your chin. If you hook it directly under your chin on a closed collar, it won't pick up your voice.

- Be careful to avoid gestures that involve tapping on your chest, and don't clap near the mike. The sound can be loud and startling.
- Fasten the battery pack to your clothing or in a pocket rather than carrying it around in your hand. It becomes a distraction to you and your audience.
- Turn the mike off completely if you're whispering something private. Don't just cover the mike. It picks up sound through your chest as well as through your lips and could broadcast words you meant for a private exchange.
- And please . . . for heaven's sake, take the mike off before you go to the restroom. No, I'm not kidding. I've overheard a few cringe-worthy moments at conferences.

If you don't have access to a lavaliere microphone, a handheld or a fixed one will have to do. A few tips for this type of mike:

- When speaking into a handheld mike, hold it like a lollipop, not an ice cream cone. Most mikes are designed to pick up sound when they're aimed right at your lips. (Think rock star.) Holding a mike daintily beneath your chin or at your chest doesn't work.
- Gesture with your non-mike hand rather than swinging the mike around. You don't want to experience the Doppler effect while you're speaking.
- Take time to adjust a fixed mike to your height. You don't want to set your stance off balance by hunching over or standing on tiptoes to reach it.

Seated Presentations

There are times when you'll present while seated, perhaps at a roundtable workshop or as part of a panel presentation. Those with physical limitations or those confined to wheelchairs present seated all the time, of course. Here are some tips for adapting the delivery skills for a seated presentation:

- Sit with your torso erect and avoid leaning on the table. (Adopt that alert/relaxed state we've discussed earlier.)
- Resist the urge to make yourself smaller by crossing your legs or wrapping your feet around your chair legs. Place your feet flat on the floor. If modesty requires it, cross your legs at the ankles; crossing at your thighs sets you off-balance and cuts off blood flow, which makes your body feel anxious even if you're not. It also sets your body on an awkward angle, causing you to tilt your shoulders and head to compensate: not a strong sitting posture.
- At the same time, avoid what has been called "man spread". (Sorry guys. It's usually men who do this.) Leaning back, resting an ankle on a knee, and resting arms

on the back of chairs may appear relaxed, but it can also come off as arrogant or disinterested.

- Gestures should still be large when seated, but rather than wide (where you might bop a fellow participant in the nose), think of putting gestures out in front of you, over the table. I think of my gesture space, while seated, as being about the size of two basketballs arranged vertically in front of me, over the table.
- Making eye contact with those directly beside you or on the same side of the table as you can be tricky. Don't leave any eye contact orphans. If you need to pull your body back now and then so you can look at the person next to you without your noses touching, it's worth it. The same is true with leaning forward to catch the eyes of those down the row, blocked by the heads of nearer participants. If you don't include these folks, their disengagement will show and their bored faces are visible to all!

Using Your Notes

A lot of people hesitate to use notes, afraid they'll look unprepared if they do. The truth is that most listeners see the use of notes as very human and as a sign that you came prepared and are staying on course. Using notes effectively will become nearly invisible to your listeners and is much better than feeling panicky or meandering aimlessly through your talk.

I mentioned earlier the advantage of one-page notes and the disadvantages of using index cards or stapled pages. Index cards and stapled pages practically guarantee problems. If your hands tremble—mine do when I'm extra nervous—held pages will broadcast the fact. It's also easy to lose your place with both cards and multiple sheets.

While you won't want to use notes in every presentation, it's often quite acceptable to have a simple map to keep your talk on track. If you have a prepared talk and you've used a Story Map to design it, that map can also serve as your notes, as we discussed in part 1. I like to make a color photocopy of my Story Map to use as my notes. I always have a pad of Post-its in my bag in case I need to make a last-minute adjustment and I can adhere a new note right to over the top of my page. This sometimes happens when I learn a particular need of the group right before I begin, or if I remembered something on the way to the venue. Sometimes that popcorn keeps popping.

Remember, I suggested that, as you practice your talk, you should trim the number of words per Post-it down to just a few, and even a simple symbol or two that will jog your memory and remind you of the prepared ideas you've practiced? Just like a map you read while driving, you want only enough detail on your notes to help you navigate, and not so much that you have to read it word for word.

To weave the use of notes into effective delivery skills, here a couple of tips:

1. Don't over-rely on your notes. If you've created your Story Map thoughtfully and practiced, you likely know your talk better than you think you do. It's a matter of self-trust at play here. Take advantage of silence and stillness for a few seconds and the image of your Story Map will often come to you.

2. Use your notes if you need them, but *really* use them. If you need to look at your notes, no harm, no foul. Just don't fake it and pretend you're *not* looking at them. If you try to sneak a peek at your notes pretending that you're not, it makes you look like a kid cheating off of his classmate's paper. You also won't get a full gulp of what you need to go on with your talk, so you'll have to keep looking again and again. Instead, remember my one and only rule: *You only get to talk to people.* Stop. Be silent. *Really* look at the notes until you know the next idea or two. Then resume eye contact and talk. Your audience will barely notice, and won't mind even if they do. Having notes and using them well, without disengaging from your listeners, makes you appear prepared . . . because you are. This also creates natural silence—always a good thing.

3. Not using notes at all. There are some kinds of talks where you won't use notes at all because it would either be awkward or unnecessary. Interviews, panel discussions, and agent pitches are examples. That doesn't mean you can't prepare an abbreviated version of a Story Map for your own benefit. Consider the preparation "back story." You may not articulate every item you've prepared, but to have it in mind can be of great assistance even in extemporaneous speaking. Preparing a Setup portion of the Story Map is exceptionally helpful in preparing for these seemingly impromptu kinds of talks. You can even use the Setup model (Connection, Conflict, Consequences/POV, Invitation, Payoff) to describe the plot of your novel, memoir, or the content of your nonfiction book. It's a nice tool to have in your pocket.

The Most Important Delivery Skill of All

In the previous pages, I provided specific behaviors—the nuts and bolts of what to do with your face, hands, voice, and body—that will enhance any speaker's delivery skills. These seemingly simple behaviors can turn a bland presentation into an interesting one, an interesting one into a dynamic one, and a dynamic presentation into a memorable and inspiring talk. These skills have been transformative, not only to me as a speaker, but to me as a person walking around in the world. Clients of mine report that the same is true for them.

As much as I'm a believer in the importance of these simple, but powerful delivery skills, one overarching skill is more important than all of them put together. That skill is *presence*.

"Be here now."
—credited to Bhagasavan Das, yogi, by Ram Dass, author of *Be Here Now*

Presence is about being fully attuned emotionally, intellectually, and physically in the moment, without anticipation of what's next or frustration about what has passed. It's this mindfulness that allows us to respond authentically and wholly to each interaction.

I'm convinced that the most vital quality for charisma is presence. Beauty is beguiling. Intellect is fascinating. Humor and pathos are engaging. But presence is a liveliness of spirit that is attractive like no other. Sometimes it's flashy, but more often it's quiet and intimate.

The most distracting and unproductive delivery skills come from failing to be fully present, in the moment. We are thinking ahead to what's coming up in our talk, and not articulating our current idea as well as we might. We are worried about how we look, sound, or the impression we are making. We fear (or perceive in an audience member's face) a negative reaction to what we're about to say. While a listener asks a question, rather than fully hearing her, we're concentrating on the time, or on the next slide we're going to show. We may wear concern on our faces about what we have already left out of our talk, while we're delivering a lighthearted portion, so our expression doesn't match our content.

In these ways, and a thousand more, it is when we are not fully present in the moment that we miss opportunities for the most poignant and powerful connections with our listeners, to be nimble and responsive to the energy in the room, to experience compassion for a listener who shares her story, and to enjoy spontaneous, organic humor that occurs in the exchange with listeners and interviewers.

Presence is the *fun* part of public speaking: the surprise encounters, the magical connection between speaker and listener, the shared moments where our humanity is entwined with others in a common experience. Presence gives us all of this.

"Be here now" is not just a book title, or a quaint, new-agey idea—it's a highly practical skill required to become a gifted public speaker. By being mindful, fully present in each moment, your face, voice, and body will be in harmony with what's happening in that moment, whether you're speaking or listening. When you're talking of being excited—if you're existing "in the moment"—you'll appear excited . . . because you *are* excited. If you're talking about heartbreak and being "in" that moment, your face and voice will convey heartbreak. The more present you are, the more natural the delivery skills will become and the less you'll have to think about them.

The more present you are, the more authentic you are. That's powerful!

Conclusion to part 3

Delivery skills cannot replace your content, but poor delivery skills can diminish the impact of what you're saying. Artfully used, delivery skills can be the magic secret sauce that lets your message and you fully emerge.

I invite you to become a keen observer. Watch prepared talks, casual exchanges, even everyday interactions as you go about your business. Observe which delivery skills you come to admire and which ones annoy you.

And practice. Experiment with your voice as you tell or read stories. Practice your neutral stance when you're waiting in line. Try using silence to reduce non-words when you speak casually. The links throughout this Delivery Skills section will let you see examples, but you can also find your own by seeking out videos and live events where you get to observe speakers of your choosing. I invite you to make note of what you learn as a knowledgeable observer.

Like the techniques of skilled writing, delivery skills are simple to learn, but take a lifetime to master. Be patient with yourself. Pick one skill at a time.

As you hone your own delivery skills, I predict that you'll find an increased confidence level along with increased effectiveness. I've found them to be transformative in my life and I'm confident that you will, too.

Make It Stick

   EXERCISE #1: APPRECIATING THE POWER OF VOICE

To gain a full appreciation for the power of the voice, enjoy one or more of the following:

- **Listen to an audiobook,** perhaps one of a book you've read before so that you can concentrate on the voice. Audiobooks can be purchased online or borrowed from most public libraries. I strongly recommend the audio version of *The Poisonwood Bible* by Barbara Kingsolver. The narration is extraordinary.

- **Tune in to National Public Radio** (or stream it online) and listen to "This American Life" or another of the storytelling programs on NPR. (More podcasts and story-reading programs are listed in the resources in the back of this book.) Make note of the vocal qualities of the storytellers and the musical devices they use with their voices. Decide which skills enhance or detract from the stories.

- **If you have little ones in your life, experiment with your voice while reading them stories.** Try for some extremes in volume, cadence, pace, rhythm, and pitch. Have fun! Listen to children's audiobooks to hear extra variety.

Read your own work aloud and record it. Listening to your reading will give you guidance about whether you need to add more dynamics to your voice as well as to hear the value of pausing. It's odd at first, but worth getting used to hearing your own voice as a learning tool.

  EXERCISE #2: APPRECIATE SILENCE

Do a Internet search and observe the following extraordinary writer/speakers to get an appreciation for pausing:

- David Whyte
- Maya Angelou
- Dorothy Allison
- Pat Conroy
- David Sedaris
- Coleman Barks

These are some my favorites. Try looking for your own favorite authors and poets. Observe their use of silence.

EXERCISE #3: A BIG STRETCH

For those who want to fully stretch their delivery skills and build self-confidence, I suggest considering taking an improvisation class through your local community college or local theater. Learning to play and to trust yourself to think on your feet can make a world of difference in your speaking ability as well as your anxiety level.

EXERCISE #4: A JUST-FOR-FUN EXAMPLE

Will Stephen delivers a delightful TED Talk that pokes fun at delivery skills clichés. It's called "How to Sound Smart in Your TED Talk." Ironically, he uses excellent delivery skills to make his points. Enjoy.

EXERCISE #5: A LITTLE SOMETHING FOR THE INTROVERTS (EXTROVERTS CAN WATCH, TOO)

Susan Cain's TED Talk "The Power of Introverts" is full of insights. Watch it for content, but also for her use of silence and other delivery skills.

EXERCISE #6: GREAT MOVIE LINES MADE GREATER

Do an Internet search for any of your favorite movie lines. (I named a few in the earlier in this chapter, but you can also find your own.) Links to video clips of these quotes almost always pops up.

- Observe how the actors bring life to the lines using their faces, voices, and bodies.
- Take special note of the actors' use of silence and how it adds dimension to the spoken words.

EXERCISE #7: GOLDEN GATE LEARNING

I have the supreme luxury of driving over the Golden Gate Bridge often, and it never ceases to amaze me, both as an engineering marvel and a work of art. The stunning saffron color of the bridge is a big part of its attraction, and that color doesn't come easy. Between the powerful winds and the salt air, the paint on the bridge corrodes quickly. Therefore, the process of painting the Golden Gate is a continuous one. They work from one end to the other over the course of many months. As soon as they reach the end, the crews move back to the beginning start again.

This is the model I invite you to use for learning the delivery skills. Pick one delivery skill. Work on it for a week. Then move to the next. Bounce back and forth between composure and delivery skills. I suggest working on sustaining eye contact whenever you're speaking to others. The other five skills, do one at a time: Stance, Silence, Animation (Movement, Gestures, Face and Voice).

Just like with the Golden Gate, when you've gone through this rotation, start it over again and repeat the cycle.

If you go through this cycle three times, you'll see huge improvement in your skills in just a couple of months.

PART 4

Transform Presentations Into Conversations

"Tell me and I forget. Teach me and I remember. Involve me and I learn."
—Attributed to Ben Franklin, Confucius, and Zun Kuang

When most people—particularly writers—think of themselves speaking in public, they tend to conjure an image of standing at a lectern talking to a group of eager listeners, all facing forward, "audience" style. The audience in this fantasy offers applause, but they're otherwise silent. This may be a description of a keynote, a commencement address, or a TED Talk, but it's not a description of the audiences most writers will have for most of their public speaking events.

Your audience can be a single interviewer on a local radio station, and by extension, her listeners. It can be a group of readers in a book club. It can be an agent or publisher to whom you pitch your book idea at a writers' conference. Your audience, even in formal settings, may be seated, facing you, but they will likely not be silent. They'll have reactions, questions, and comments, some asked as part of your presentation, others afterward in a one-on-one exchange. Writer talks and readings are not just "presentations," they're conversations. And that is good.

While speakers spend lots of time thinking (and sometimes fretting) about what they're going to say in a presentation, they typically spend very little time preparing for how to invite, welcome, and manage interaction, including challenging questions from their listeners. When faced with challenging questions or pushback on their ideas, they feel intimidated, surprised, and unprepared. They can get flustered, defensive, or divulge things they later wish they hadn't.

Public speaking for writers is seldom a monologue, and we don't want it to be. If prepared for and managed with skill, tough questions—even the occasional obnoxious ones—can be golden opportunies to build connections and to demonstrate new levels of skill, knowledge, and personal aplomb. Without preparation, such questions can be our undoing, can reduce our credibility, and can just feel crummy, even making us never want to speak in public again.

As I teach the simple tools for preparing for, eliciting, and managing interaction with listeners in the coming pages, I'll ask you to recall interviews you've watched, heard, or been part of, and to observe with new eyes as you watch new interviews. What qualities do you appreciate in an interviewer? As a listener or audience member, what do you like to see or hear in the exchange between interviewer and interviewee? What kinds of interviewees' responses pique your interest and make you want to learn more about them and their ideas? What turns you off? What makes you want to go buy their books?

By learning a few simple techniques and tools—and practicing a bit—we can prepare ourselves to make the most of interviews, to come across with the same authenticity we aim for in our presentations, and to manage challenging questions, and occasionally challenging people, with grace.

Here we'll cover:

- Creating room for and inviting interaction with attitude and time management.
- Managing challenging questions, challenging interactions, and challenging people by taking the "LEAD" of interaction.
- Adapting the Story Map and LEAD techniques to prepare for interviews and pitches when you're not in control of the flow of content.

CHAPTER 17

Create Room for Interaction

*A single conversation across the table with a
wise person is worth a month's study of books.*
—Chinese Proverb

U p to this point, I've offered you skills (along with a little cheerleading) that encourage your confidence. I've prodded you not to make yourself small, to take up room with your body, your voice, and your ideas. Here, we'll make a turn. Part 4 is about making room for others in your presentation. Whether they participate verbally, physically, or silently, your listeners' involvement is crucial. I still stand by my encouragement of you to take up room—just don't take up all of it. Making room for listeners is vital to the success of every talk, to say nothing of your own enjoyment of it. It's often in our exchanges with listeners that we get a 3-D perspective of our story's impact on listeners.

There are two elements to creating room for interaction: The first is creating a welcoming attitude toward questions and push-back, the second is building time and opportunity for listeners to voice their questions, concerns, and make contributions to the topic.

When I ask my clients how they're preparing to answer aggressive opposition, pushback, or challenging questions, they usually say something like, "I'm just hoping nobody asks about *that*, for heaven's sake!"

Hoping not to be asked a tough question is not a strategy. In fact, it's the opposite of a strategy. I recommend that you hope *for* such questions. Time for another mental shift.

Adjusting Your Attitude to Create Room for Interaction

"The biggest problem with communication is the illusion that it has taken place."
—George Bernard Shaw

Speakers who are excessively nervous about challenging interactions often either consciously or unconsciously preclude interaction from occurring. They deliver their presentation as a monologue rather than allowing for dialogue. They over pack their talks with so much content that there's no time to field questions. They don't call on those who might offer challenge. They offer indirect or non-answers to unsettling questions they'd rather not answer. They start packing up their belongings—stacking papers, gathering their pens—while they're finishing their talks, implying with their bodies that interaction is unwelcome. (Yes, I've witnessed this many times and too often at author events.) All these actions say the same thing: *Don't ask!*

Challenging questions and pushback give presenters big gifts of opportunity. The trick is to recognize them as the gifts they are:

- **They reveal misunderstandings.** Listeners may be confused or may misinterpret what you've said. Their questions allow you to provide clarity or correction on the spot. Sometimes we're not as clear as we assume.
- **They remind you of something you left out of your talk.** Whether you forgot to include an idea in the design of your talk or you accidentally left it out, a question or comment from listeners may jog your memory and give you a second chance to include it. Win, win.
- **They offer an opportunity for you to reveal more depth.** Questions and comments let you go deeper on a topic than your prepared remarks might have. This lets you expand, offer more detail or examples, and reveal a greater depth of knowledge, insight, or experience to your listeners.

- **They make for more intimate and organic connection to listeners.** How you manage a tough question or a challenging audience member gives you a chance to demonstrate confidence, empathy, humor, and grace. You can defend your position without getting defensive. You can disagree without being disagreeable. You can hold your ground, but do so with respect for those who object.
- **They add another dimension to your talk.** I approach every talk assuming there is wisdom in the room, not only in my own mind. Many times, challenges and interaction from your listeners add unexpected depth to your talk. Their stories, examples, and concerns may add more value to the conversation, applying what you're sharing to their circumstances. If you're addressing a controversial topic, it may it a story from an audience member that makes the point to his peers in the room, sometimes even better than you'd be able to do so.
- **The question or opinion may be more universal than you know.** Just because only one person asks a question or issues a challenge, doesn't mean she's the only one with that question or concern. By answering the questions one person asks, you are likely answering the same question for many others who might not have voiced it.
- **They are far better voiced than silent.** As uncomfortable as it may seem to face public opposition to your ideas or get challenged about your writing, it is far better to have the opportunity to address these issues than to have them go "underground." Unvoiced, you are without a chance to have an opportunity to influence listeners' assumptions.
- **They are often legitimate and valuable questions that deserve answers.** While we'll address different kinds of questions and questioners in a bit, it's worth saying that many, if not most, challenging questions come from a valid need to have them answered. If your topic is worth talking about, it's worth exploring and that means welcoming challenges. Wear your thicker skin.
- **They are an inevitable byproduct of your own bold POV.** The stronger your POV and the more controversial or revolutionary your ideas, the higher the likelihood of being challenged. Rather than dread it, take challenges as evidence that your topic is important and that is challenging the thinking and attitudes of your listeners. A strong POV is disruptive. Art is, by its very nature, disruptive. This is part of the job of writers, so it's wise to prepare for some opposition.

When questions are straightforward and you are comfortable giving a straightforward answer, there's little need for me to offer coaching. Some questions are not so benign and some interaction with listeners is not in the form of questions at all, but stories they tell, opinions they offer, and comments they make. A few types of audience members that are trickier to manage:

- **The pontificator** who has no real question, but dominates the allotted time with her own long-winded stories that may or may not have anything to do with the topic you're addressing.
- **The "devil's advocate"** who feels the need to oppose your statements . . . just because.
- **The "ozone questioner"** is someone who asks questions, seemingly from outer space, which are at best tangential to the topic at hand.
- **The expert** who isn't just contributing to the talk, but competing with you to be seen as more knowledgeable about your topic, whether or not she actually is.
- **The stinker/heckler.** Sorry, folks, but some people can just be obnoxious. It's not common for most author talks, but it does happen that the occasional stinker speaks up, particularly if your topic is provocative. Still, you want to manage these folks with grace and not with antagonism.
- **The provocateur.** Now and then any speaker might face a question from a listener that's vulgar, inappropriate, and seems designed to embarrass. These are rare for most authors, but they can come up now and then.

MENTAL SHIFT

Objections are good news.
Rather than seeing opposition to your ideas as bad, I encourage you to see them as evidence of listener engagement and an opportunity for you to show more of what you know and what you're made of. Art is meant to disrupt thinking. If you're getting opposition to your ideas, it may just mean you're on the right track and that you've engaged the curiosity and emotions of your listeners.

If you begin to see challenges to your ideas—as the mental shift above suggests—as both evidence of interest and as opportunity to go deeper, you'll be less inclined to avoid them. Even if a question seems hostile or aggressive, even if the person asking it is a bit of a jerk, it's incumbent upon the speaker to treat the questioner with respect. After all, you invited her to the party. This does not mean that you cede your presentation to a blowhard. Not at all! Using the tool I'll cover in a bit, you can hold your ground, defend your position, and manage difficult people without letting them take over or dominate.

Of course, in a heated political climate or when speaking on a highly controversial subject, there is the rare, but possible risk of an audience member becoming overly hostile, or even dangerous. I often speak on topics related to suicide and gun violence and I know that people have strong feelings about this and that reactions can be intense. I'm not suggesting that these skills eliminate danger if someone is armed, though they can cool hot tensions between sensible people. If you're tackling hot-button issues, please take appropriate precautions.

My experience tells me this: whenever a speaker gets into a combative verbal exchange with an audience member, it's the speaker who loses—one hundred percent of the time. Snapping back with a smarty-pants answer to a heckler is fine for comedians in nightclubs. It's my experience, though, that for presentations to celebrate books or to inform or inspire listeners, that such a tug-of-war rarely benefits the speaker. It makes him appear anything but composed and confident. It can make him seem like a bully. It's better to use the LEAD technique that I'll cover shortly than to get into a war of words with an audience member.

Manage Time to Invite Interaction

I'm sure you now see why you should welcome challenges from listeners. Now, let's address how to get them to want to interact.

The first step is to leave enough time for interaction. When we addressed the Story Map in part 2, I cautioned about over packing. I recommended preparing content for only about two-thirds of the time you have for a presentation of less than an hour, or in each module of a daylong workshop-style presentation. If you cram content in right up to the last moments of your talk, listeners will feel as though they can't—or worse, don't want to—ask questions. By preparing less content, you're creating space for listeners to interact. You can also let your listeners know that you'll have time at the end for questions, that you'll stop several times throughout to welcome their input, or that you'd prefer they interrupt along the way for a truly conversational style. It's up to you. Just pick the format that works best for your topic, audience, and goal, and build it into your time. To do this, of course, you will need time practicing your talk to know how much time it'll really take to deliver. Trim it. Edit it. Less is more.

Silence can invite questions. What many speakers do is ask for questions, wait less than a nanosecond, then say, "Thanks so much. If there are no questions, I'd like to thank you for coming."

By inviting questions then inserting a few seconds of silence, you allow your listeners to formulate their questions or ideas. This moment invites more thoughtful questions rather than just hopping onto the first hand that goes up. The silence also implies you really want the interaction—rather than having asked out of obligation—and that you have time for your listeners to talk. *Silence is the most important tool for converting a presentation into a conversation.*

Mary Budd Rowe, a master educator, wrote in 1972 about "wait time," a concept respected by educators to this day. She suggested that waiting one to three seconds after asking a question of students of any age solicits a significantly higher engagement level and a higher quality of answer. Using "wait time" when you're either inviting questions or asking them of your listeners will serve the same way. Invite questions and then—wait for it—wait a little longer. Silence will prompt your listeners, elegantly cueing them that it's their turn. If you've left room in the timeframe and used a few seconds of wait time, you're much more likely to get a richer and more valuable level of exchange. You'll be surprised at just how powerful pausing is.

Silence—I'm a big fan.

In this chapter, we talked about inviting questions and comments from listeners. In the next chapter, we'll address what to do once you get a challenging question.

CHAPTER 18

Manage Challenging Interactions
by Taking the LEAD

I just spent the last chapter talking about how to invite and make room for interaction—questions and comments from your audience members. But what about when you get a tough question? You don't want to be like a dog chasing a school bus with absolutely no plan for what to do if you catch it.

Handling Challenging Questions with Grace

Challenging questions at a live event can feel intimidating. Occasionally, they're intended to be. Such question may make us angry, embarrassed, or confused. We have an intense urge to answer fast so that we don't look as though we don't know the answer. It's not a gunfight; it's a conversation. There's no reward for being quick on the draw with your reply. Answering too quickly can make you appear panicky or defensive (even if you're not), and matching hostility with hostility nearly always reduces your credibility. What's worse is that answering quickly, before you've given yourself a chance to reflect, can result in an impulsive, rather than a thoughtful reply.

Remember earlier when I talked about setting the "climate" in a room. Here's where it's important to regulate the temperature. If the question is hot, cool it off with your soothing composure skills and with a "cool" tone of voice. You don't want anybody to get burned.

There are presenters, including some authors, who choose an abrasive, combative, or antagonistic style. Some politicians and pundits are intentionally combative, as are some edgier comedians and authors. If that meets their goals, it's fine. Most of us prefer not to fight with our listeners; we want to connect with them. For most of us, handling interactions with some elegance serves us better than fighting. When you're tossed a tough question or comment, the model below will help keep you cool, keep you from appearing defensive, and allow your listeners to respect your management of a difficult interaction.

When a question is challenging, highly emotional, incendiary, intrusive, rude, or inappropriate, don't just answer it out of impulse or a knee-jerk reaction—*LEAD* the exchange. I'll teach you the principles, then follow with some examples for clarity.

STEP 1: LISTEN TO THE QUESTION

"I'm a very strong believer in listening and learning from others."
—Ruth Bader Ginsberg, Supreme Court Justice

Plenty of presentations go south during the Q&A because of a simple lack of listening on the part of the presenter. I once witnessed a speaker who had over packed her content and run nearly up to her time limit. She had time for only one question and it was a doozy. It clearly intimidated the speaker so much that she barely listened to the question, then she jumped in with her answer to the question she *thought* she was being asked—I'm guessing it was a question she dreaded—and it wasn't what was being asked at all. When she finished, that same questioner clarified the very benign question he was asking, one that the speaker was happy to entertain. Because she hadn't tuned in, the speaker was in the weeds, unnecessarily dealing with topics she didn't want to manage.

When someone is asking a question, *listen*.

No, *really* listen. She may not be asking what you fear; she may not be asking what you think she's asking. Let her voice the entire question before you butt in and answer what you think she's asking. This is tricky when it's a question you've been asked many times, particularly if it's one that gets under your skin. Remember, this is the first time *this* person asked the question of you. He doesn't know you hear it all the time. To listen to him and let him voice his question or idea is a demonstration of respect and an opportunity for you to let the question soak in while you formulate your most thoughtful answer. It also lets you cool down, get your heart rate down, and get a little perspective.

"Don't take anything personally."
—Don Miguel Ruiz, author of *The Four Agreements*

It's hard not to take a challenging question personally. Writing is an intimate art form where we invite readers into our thoughts and imagination. Chances are high that if a listener has a strong, or even hostile, reaction to the content of your book or your talk, that the reaction is more about them than you. Recalling this thought helps me to "cool down."

Listen *under* the question for: skepticism, confusion, curiosity, disappointment, anger, frustration, distrust, pain, worry, fear, or philosophical disagreement.

Rather than letting myself think *What a jerk!* when I get a seemingly snarky or aggressive question, I try to think this: *Why would a reasonable, rational person ask that question? What might be going on for her?*

This requires a deeper kind of listening. If your story or your presentation has made a deep emotional connection, you may find that your listeners bring their own experience to the exchange. That's what we hope for as writers. You want intimate connection. If someone is generous enough to share her emotional truth, it deserves to be honored and heard.

"There is nothing more intimate in life than simply to be understood and to understand someone else."
—Brad Meltzer, author of *The Inner Circle*

At my memoir launch events, I addressed issues of grief and loss, and read touching and "sweet-bitter" excerpts about becoming a second mother to a son whose birth mother had died when he was small. Naturally, people had their own stories of loss, as well as questions about how we coped as a family. Building in time for interaction, not rushing them, not interrupting, and listening deeply was a huge part of welcoming the stories that others brought to mine. It created an atmosphere of intimacy and connection. This was one of the most satisfying 3-D experiences of sharing my book. The stories of others added greater dimension to my story, and the bonds formed in those brief exchanges made the writing of my book feel more valuable.

STEP 2: EMPATHIZE

Before you rush to answer a challenging question, there's an important first step. Your questioners may not overtly voice the emotional heat in their questions, so you'll have to listen for tone, watch their faces, wonder what's behind the question. You may even need to ask them to clarify or to say more so that you understand. When you get the sense that you know the emotion they're conveying, empathize with it. The empathy should be genuine and specific. "Wow, I can see how hard that would be," or, "If I was in your shoes, I'd wonder the same thing."

Avoid "canned" empathic responses. You know what I mean if you've ever called a customer service line with a complaint (and a fair bit of frustration) and gotten a response that feels as though they're reading it off of a card, delivered in a robotic voice. *We are so sorry you're experiencing this difficulty...* Aaaagh! It makes me want to scream into the phone. To be authentic in our empathy requires that "be here now" presence we talked about earlier.

Here are a few tips to help with the "empathize" step of this tool. Of course, tone of voice, facial expression, and body posture can radically enhance or contradict your empathic response. Most crucial of all is that you are authentic in your empathy.

- **Empathy does not mean agreement.** You can care about the emotional experience of your listener without agreeing with either her premise or her challenge to your content. If she says something like, *I've tried that a thousand times and it never works,* you don't want to validate that it doesn't work, of course. Instead you might empathize. *What I'm proposing isn't easy and I understand that lot of folks have tried and struggled. I did, too, at first.* See, you're empathizing, but not agreeing.

  Empathy says, *I hear you.* It says, *I get it,* or *I'm trying to.* It says, *I can understand why you might feel that way even if I don't feel that way.* Empathy cools the question from hot to warm and allows you to answer—even passionately disagree—without alienating your guest.

  If you disagree, empathize first, and then state that you disagree. For example: *I understand that many people have held that belief for a very long time.* (Pause.) *Let me tell you why I now disagree.* See, you've heard, you've empathized, and you have another point of view on the matter, backed up with some experience or data. This helps to eliminate an argument with your listener.

  Disagreeing with your listeners does not mean you argue with them. It just means that you respect that they have a different idea than yours. Empathizing, followed with your statement that you disagree is different than arguing.

- **Resist using disqualifiers.** Once you've voiced empathy, and before you move on to give your answer, there's an important pitfall to avoid: disqualifying language. Often between empathizing with the questioner's emotions and answering, speakers articulate a word or phrase that undoes the empathy completely.

The most frequently used disqualifying word is "but." My mother once told me that anything spoken after the word "but" is a lie. Obviously that's not true when "but" is used as a simple conjunction and not 100% of the other times either, but in crucial moments, Ma was onto something.

I understand, BUT . . . (I'm about to say something that indicates I don't really understand.)
I don't want to hurt your feelings, BUT . . . (I'm about to say something hurtful.)
I'm not racist, BUT . . . (I'm about to say something that will sound or be racist.)
I'm sorry, BUT . . . (I'm about to tell you how right I am.)
I love you, BUT . . . (Duck! Something not so loving is on its way.)

"But" has its place—*not* following a statement of empathy. The word "however" is just "but" in a tuxedo. "Nevertheless" is "but" in a tiara. All of them dilute or erase the value of the empathic statement that preceded them. This technique has proven beneficial to couples in my therapy practice as well. It helps in our intimate exchanges, too.

Rather than use one of these disqualifying conjunctions, state your empathy, then employ silence. Insert an extended silence so that your listeners can absorb the authenticity of your empathy. This cools him off and paves the way for you to state your answer, even your opposition to his position.

I completely understand that your experience has made you wary of the idea that I'm proposing. (SILENCE) Here's why I believe you should entertain the idea again, despite your misgivings. (SILENCE)

This is far better than, *I completely understand, **but** you should entertain this idea anyway.*

Use of silence following a statement of empathic connection is artful and requires practice. That "but" or "however" will slip out, believe me. These qualifiers are so ubiquitous that we barely notice them. Chances are you won't even hear them when you say them. If you have a partner, a close friend, a toddler, a teenager, or a roommate, trust me, you will be given ample opportunity to practice expressing empathy toward them and their pushback on your ideas. You can use this as practice opportunity. LEAD the exchange: **Listen** and **Empathize** (using silence, no "but") before you **Answer**.

STEP 3: ANSWER

Empathy is invaluable, but it's not an answer. Do answer the question if you can.

Often people face uncomfortable questions by not answering them. Instead they swing back to whatever talking point they want to address, dismissing the question completely. Not only this is poor Q&A strategy, it's also just plain rude and risks making listeners angrier. Politicians and business leaders whom I've coached find it shocking that I won't let them get away with skirting an answer and banging a prepared talking point instead. It's better to address the question directly than sound as though you're avoiding it. You gain the respect of your listeners this way.

If you've listened to the question and empathized with the questioner, it's time to offer an answer. Perhaps it's a reiteration or clarification of something you've already said. Perhaps it's new information that you didn't cover. Answer concisely, but answer.

If you don't know the answer, that's your answer. "Gosh, I just haven't thought of it that way before. I don't really know about that. I'd have to put some thought into it."

You can sometimes "answer" by tossing it to the group. "What do the rest of you think? Perhaps you've had experiences like this." I never toss the question out to avoid the question; that would be disingenuous. I do include the other listeners if I think that it would benefit from discussion, rather than me just saying *I don't know.* Remember, there's often wisdom in the room.

It's also perfectly legitimate to follow a genuinely authentic statement of empathy with, *I don't know the answer to your question. I wish I did. What I do know is this. . .* Such an answer communicates that you heard the question, you're not evading it, but you simply do not know. It also says that just because you don't know that particular answer, your POV is still valid and you have depth of knowledge on the topic.

If there's a question you don't want to answer, it's perfectly okay not to, but do it with intention. You can empathize, then follow the empathy statement *I can understand why you're curious about that. Lots of people are,* with, *I choose not to answer questions about my kids in public. They've sworn me to secrecy.* This could even be a playful dodge. Just don't pretend you're answering a question when you're not. It lowers your credibility.

STEP 4: ADD DETAIL

To keep your Q&A from feeling like a ping-pong game of back-and-forth, I advise adding a new layer of detail to your answer.

Challenging questions are often an opportunity for you to make an answer more vivid, to give it more impact and memorability. This is a good time to include a Spellbinder: a story, research data, an example, a bit of humor, a personal disclosure, or a metaphor to make things clearer. The details you add will often tie back to either your POV, the Payoff, or more about the Connection/Challenge/Consequences parts of your Setup.

Rather than tough questions being a volley between you and a listener, they can be an opportunity for you to show facility with broadening, deepening, or richening the conversation, showing that the well of knowledge and insight from which you draw is deep. Adding more detail and possibly Spellbinders as part of your managing questions will help you toward this goal.

A Personal Story in Which I Blew It

Many years ago, in my capacity as a substance-abuse therapist at a non-profit counseling agency, I gave a talk to a local service organization on the topic of drug use in local schools. It was a community talk and a fundraising event for the agency I worked for at the time. This organization was a big donor.

During the Q&A section of my talk, a particularly insistent audience member kept pressing me to name which high school in the county had the biggest drug use problem among its students. Not only did I not want to name a particular school for political reasons, there wasn't one. Drug abuse was a serious concern in every high school in the county. I kept repeating this as fact, but the listener was persistent and I was less skilled then at managing such pushback. I was frustrated. I felt embarrassed and intimidated. He was many years older than I, and a county supervisor who had big influence over funding. As an attempt to use humor to deflect the question (and without thinking it through), I said (in a tone I intended to be playful, but that came off as snarky) *Tell you what. If you find a drug-free school in this county, I'll turn all of my furniture around and worship in that direction.* Nervous laughter rolled through the room.

I know . . . yikes. And double yikes because my flippant remark could be offensive to some religious and cultural groups. Triple yikes because I had no idea that a reporter was in the room. The *only* quote she printed from my talk in the next day's paper was that ridiculous, accidental Spellbinder. My spell turned to dark magic in that moment. That colorful detail did not further my message about all of the vital services my agency provided to the community. This is what happens when we let ourselves get pushed into a response.

Using humor is not necessarily a bad idea to take some of the steam out of an aggressive questioner, but when I was pushed into this, I went sarcastic, revealing my irritation. A better choice might have been to be playful but not sarcastic. I was clearly not in the "LEAD" of that interaction.

If I could turn back the clock, here's how I might field that question today using the LEAD method:

- **Listen:** I'd listen not only for the questioner's content, but for the underlying emotion of what he was asking. Yes, he was a bit of a stinker, but still. Thinking back, his emotion was "concern" about the community and "curiosity" about where would be the safest place for students, perhaps his own kids or grandkids.

- **Empathize:** Rather than just repeating myself and sounding defensive, I'd offer a statement of genuine empathy. *I so wish I could tell you that there is a certain school that's safe or that the problem of drug use is isolated to a certain school. We all want that for our kids. (SILENCE)* Let that empathy soak in. Let the other audience members feel it, too.
- **Answer:** Rather than my flippant reply, I'd state my genuine response to his concern: *Sadly, my experience tells me that drug use is present in every school, in every socio-economic class. It doesn't discriminate on the basis of gender, race, or intellect, and it certainly doesn't respect one school over another. We all wish it were an isolated problem.*
- **Detail:** Here I'd embrace the opportunity to elaborate on my POV or to give information that helped me to meet the goal of my talk, which was to thank these donors and to secure future funding from them. *Let me tell you about the programs we have in each high school, and a specific story of a student whose life has been changed because of the contributions of this service club.* (Then I'd relay the example without breaching confidentiality.)

By taking the LEAD of this interaction—rather than being pushed into an answer I didn't want to give—I would have demonstrated respect, empathy, knowledge level, and grace under pressure. If only I could time travel back to that moment.

MENTAL SHIFT

Silence is beyond golden.

Often, people fear that if they take a few seconds of silence when someone shoots a tough question at them that they'll appear as though they don't know the answer or that they lack confidence. The truth is the exact opposite.

Taking a couple of seconds when meeting a challenge gives your audience (of whatever size) the impression that you're listening and contemplating, and not reacting out of reflex rather than being thoughtful in your response. During the silence you get to breathe, cool down, and consider your response. It works for you. It works for your listeners.

Learn from my past error. Take your time. Take the LEAD. The hotter the question, the more you want to let your reaction cool off before you respond. Use silence to reflect.

"I'd rather have questions that cannot be answered than answers that can't be questioned."

—Richard Feynman, author and American physicist

Managing "That Guy"

My brother-in-law is a gregarious fellow who easily strikes up conversations with strangers he encounters. His adult kids have coined the term "that guy" to describe whatever person their dad is chatting up while they're on family outings or vacations. *Oh, let's go on to lunch, Dad's talking to "that guy."* It's family shorthand.

Here I appropriate the "that guy" tag to describe a different kind of exchange and to describe one of those people (irrespective of gender) who needs to be managed during a presentation. She's the one who needs to pontificate, or play devil's advocate, or challenge your every idea. He's the one who needs to interrupt frequently or tell long stories about his experience, taking more time than is appropriate, adding no value. She sidetracks the talk. He's a competitor, rather than a listener. Some questions border on heckling. If you've written a controversial book, you may get these now and then.

Often "that guy" is benign and can be managed with this LEAD technique. Sometimes you have to step it up a notch and interrupt.

If someone is going on and on or asking irrelevant or inappropriate questions, you can say something like, *"Please forgive me for interrupting. I see that you've got lots to say about this topic. I'd like to offer others the chance to ask questions and to honor the time limitation we have. I'd be happy to talk with you individually after the session."*

When I get an "ozone" question—not at all relevant to the topic and a distraction—I sometimes say something like, *I can understand why that's a big concern and I share it with you. I wish we had the luxury of time to explore that topic. For now, I prefer to stick to the agenda that we have before us.*

Managing a listener like this isn't always necessary and should be used rarely. I'm glad to have the skill when I need it, though, and I use it only after someone has repeatedly attempted to dominate—when she's "that guy."

Managing "that guy" isn't rude; it's respectful of your other listeners (who are often cringing and hoping "that guy" will pipe down), and it's self-respectful—a way to honor yourself, your preparation, and the other listeners. While you want to include others in the exchange, you do not want to cede your entire presentation to someone who's domineering. You're the captain—don't give up your ship!

Managing interaction, like so many other aspects of conversation, is about achieving balance. We want to welcome the input, questions, and points of view of our listeners, and we want to hold our ground. We sometimes need to defend our positions, but we don't want to become defensive. We sometimes must disagree with our listeners, even passionately, but we don't want to be disagreeable.

Preparing for Difficult Questions

In part 2, I used as a sample the Story Map that Catherine Marshall-Smith prepared for her California book launch of *American Family*. Given that the topics in her book were same-sex marriage, child custody, and evangelical Christianity, you can imagine that Catherine anticipated (and was concerned about) resistance to her topics from both strangers and familiars. She also knew that her audience and their sensibilities might be different in the San Francisco Bay Area than in some of other locations she'd be talking as she promoted her book. As is often the case, Catherine rarely faced the hot opposition that she feared. Still, it's good to be prepared. You never know.

Rather than just hoping they won't occur, I ask my clients to prepare for challenging questions and push back on their topics. To prepare Catherine for challenging questions, we "popcorned" all of the ones she feared most, writing them one at a time onto Post-its. Then we let a few others pop. I offered a few. It's often helpful to ask input from someone else when you're trying to imagine possible challenging questions.

We practiced, using the LEAD model so that Catherine got a few of those answers in her mind, on her lips, and down into her bones. She faced less opposition than she anticipated, as is often the case, but she felt better prepared for having taken the time to practice the toughies.

To prepare for Q&A, you can use the same Post-it method I recommended for crafting your content. Put one tough question on a Post-it. Then write out and practice your LEAD response: **Listen, Empathize, Answer,** add **Detail.**

Most of the questions you'll face as an author will be curious, interesting, and well-intended. Of course, we can never anticipate every question we'll face. Nevertheless, it's valuable to anticipate the questions that might be most provocative based on our topic or our audience, and to have a method—in this case LEAD—for fielding unexpected questions or challenging audience members.

The Dumb Question

Haven't we all heard the old saw that there are no dumb questions? At risk of sounding rude, I disagree.

When I was in high school I worked in a roller-rink snack bar. (Yes, on skates.) A man came to the snack bar, looked up at the menu with a furrowed brow, then with no hint of irony asked,

How much are your thirty-five-cent Cokes? I replied, *Fifty cents*. It seemed like a dumb question and I couldn't resist. He would have paid it had I not fessed up to my silliness. We shared a laugh. He was not a dumb guy, but it *was* a dumb question.

Occasionally you'll get a dumb question, either because the person spaced out and didn't hear something properly, didn't think it through, or for a host of other reasons. Listeners get confused, misunderstand, or voice some odd or tangential thought that seems silly. Who among us hasn't uttered a stupid question now and then? Some speakers make big fun of an audience member for asking one of these "dumb" questions. Again, this may be fine for a comedian handling a heckler, but it's not such a great strategy for author talks. To me, embarrassing an audience member who bothered to ask a question makes the speaker look like a bully. In very hot controversy, it could spark something worse. Better to cool things down than heat them up.

I don't want anyone at any event where I'm speaking to feel humiliated by me. They're honoring me by being willing to sit in an audience and listen. When they utter a dumb (or seemingly dumb) question, and the rest of the audience giggles, I don't want to pile on. Instead, I'll rescue them. *Hey, I know that sounded a little silly to some of you, but there's an important point in there that I'd like to address.* I listen for the emotion of the question so that I can empathize with that part. I use my seconds of silence to look for kernels of value in even the most absurd questions. I try to listen past what might seem dumb about it for an opportunity to offer information, insight, and to demonstrate some decency toward my listener. Nobody likes being embarrassed in public. I try not to let it happen to anybody on my watch.

ONE IMPRESSIVE EXAMPLE

A viral video that illustrates a great way to handle a wildly inappropriate question made the rounds. Lauren Conrad is an actor who was a guest on a morning radio program called "Sway in the Morning." Questions for the guests are written down and pulled randomly. Conrad reports that she doesn't know if the questions are from listeners, the host, or staff. She was there to talk about her TV show and her acting, but was faced with a particularly vulgar, inappropriate "from the hat" question asking about her "favorite position." Though the question was obviously meant as sexual innuendo, Conrad paused, breathed, and responded by saying, "CEO. That's my favorite position."

In this case, because the question was intentionally inappropriate, it deserved no empathy. Instead, Conrad went straight at it. Rather than letting the question fluster her, she took her time and formed an answer that outsmarted the questioner. Her cleverness outshone the vulgarity and inappropriateness of the question. Brava!

Eye Contact during Q&A: Share the Love

When an audience member asks a question, it's tempting to have a one-on-one conversation with just that person. If it's a very brief question with a concise answer, that's not a problem. If the question is a challenging one that requires a longer LEAD response, that conversation can be perceived as a private party to which the rest of the audience is not invited.

To remedy this, look at the questioner while you're listening and during your statement of empathy. Then, share the love. By this I mean, go back to your usual way of distributing eye contact around the room. This includes everybody in the conversation. Remember, if one person asked the question, more might be wondering about it.

By welcoming and preparing for interaction, writers experience some of the richest opportunities to promote their books. They also enjoy one of the most soul-satisfying aspects of talking about their writing in public, that 3-D moment when they get to hear and feel their listeners' experiences of their stories. By employing the LEAD techniques, writers can defend their positions without getting defensive, welcome opposition without alienating, and forge a closer connection with their listeners.

Make It Stick

EXERCISE #1: THE GOOD, THE BAD, AND THE UGLY

Observe Q&A on a topic of controversy. I invite you to tune into a political panel news program, or attend a local town hall meeting when a heated topic is being addressed. (It won't be hard to find one.) Make note of how the speakers and subject matter experts manage questions.

- Do people seem to listen? Do you hear empathy? Do they answer the questions?
- What do you notice about body posture, facial expressions, and tone of voice when someone is fielding a tough question?
- What is the impact of those on you as a listener?

EXERCISE #2: FRIENDS AND FAMILY

Next time you're having a disagreement (a low-key one, please) with a loved one whose position differs from yours, try to use the LEAD technique rather than simply repeating your point or escalating the exchange. Try slowing it down. Observe the results.

CHAPTER 19

Preparing for Interviews When You're
Not in Control of the Flow

*"It usually takes me more than three weeks to prepare a
good impromptu speech."*
—Mark Twain

If you've done some good marketing of your book or an article you've written on a topic of your expertise or passion, you may be fortunate enough to be offered interviews by print reporters, radio or TV hosts, podcasters, or as a member of a panel discussion with a moderator and an audience asking questions. As scary as this might sound to newbie speakers, interviews are golden opportunities for more people to learn about your writing, about you, and about whatever causes or ideas you're promoting. It pays to prepare.

What do we do to prepare content for an interview? How can you prepare answers when you don't know the questions?

Prior to thinking about your specific answers to possible questions, it pays to prepare for interviews just as you would for a prepared talk. Back in part 2 when we discussed the Story Map, remember the questions you asked before preparing your content: *What's my topic? What's my goal? Who are my listeners? What are the logistics of the event?*

These questions are equally relevant when preparing for an interview, though there's a bit of adaptation because—guess what—you're not in control of the itinerary of your interviewer. Your book and your background are the general topics, but some interviewers want to focus on a specific aspect of your story, either because of their personal interests or because their program has a particular focus. Your interviewer is one listener; her audience makes up the rest of the listeners. It's important to keep both in mind.

Interview Preparation

- **Communicate with the host.** If you get to talk or exchange email with the host of the program or a panel moderator beforehand, they'll sometimes share the kinds of questions they'll ask. Not always, but it's worth asking. If you employ a publicist, this is something she will likely do on your behalf. Interviewers may still switch topics up, but it'll help to know a bit going in. You can also plant seeds about what you think would be a good angle to discuss.

- **Don't assume every host has read your book.** It sounds odd, but it's true. I'd say about 50 percent of the people who interviewed me about my books had either read only part of the book, or none of it, prior to the interview. Knowing this possibility, you may need to take more of the lead of the discussion, guiding the interviewer to topics you want to discuss.

- **For media interviews, send a press packet that includes a preferred-topics list.** Interviewers welcome these. They don't always stick to them, but it's often a good starting point.

- **Listen to the program.** Radio, TV, and podcast hosts often have archives of past interviews. It's to your advantage to get to know that host before your interview. Listen to one or several interviews to get a notion of the style of your host, and the kinds of subject matter to which he gravitates. You may gather a tidbit or two about the host and his interests that helps you make a connection.

- **Make note of biases and the focus of a show.** Some hosts hold strong points of view and a deep, personal attachment to a theme. Their followers often share that. While you'd never change your book or your own values to please a host, it is worth knowing those tendencies before your interview. You might choose a different aspect of your story to share with a program that has a psychology focus versus one with a political bent. Customize. Consider the host and her audience.

- **Sometimes, sit one out.** Some programs or hosts may not be suited to the topics you talk or write about. In our desperation for book publicity, we sometimes feel that we should take every opportunity. If you cannot comfortably adapt your topic to suit the listenership or a particular host, or if the program seems antithetical to your values, skipping it might be wise.

- **Select two or three super-short (maybe one- to two-minute) excerpts that you could read from your book, if asked.** Have them marked or printed out. You may use one, two, or none of these, but it's better than scrambling and leafing through your book to find one if the host asks you to read. Pick dynamic, active passages, not long narrative and descriptive passages. These will be much more engaging for listeners.

- **Visit in person if you can.** If your radio or podcast interviewer is within a reasonable driving distance and the host is open to it, I advise going to the studio rather than calling into the station for your interview. In person, you get to have eye contact and make a warmer connection with the host. Plus, it's fun. Of course, if you are fortunate enough to land a big interview on a major network, traveling (even at your expense) might be worth it, or some networks might pay your travel expenses. This is a unicorn of an opportunity for other than the most elite of authors, but, hey—it could happen!

- **Employ animation in your voice.** Without any visuals to rely on in a radio or podcast interview, you have only your voice to make connection with your interviewer and with listeners. Remember your storytelling voice, that voice you might use to read to little kids. Use animation and variation of tone, volume, pace, and rhythm to add interest.

- **Get there *early*.** Whether you're going in person to a studio or you're calling into a radio or podcast show, arrive substantially early. You want to be calm, not rushed. If you're calling in, don't wait until the last minute. Make sure you've already downloaded whatever program they require, such as Skype or Zoom. Know that technology can fail. Give yourself time enough to try a second or third time in case connections don't work.

- **Don't multitask.** If you're calling into a program, focus on the conversation at hand. Turn off your phone's ringer. Set your cell phone out of view. Don't answer a text. Don't type. (I've heard typing during a couple of radio interviews and podcasts. *Gack!*) Get someone to mind the kids and the dog. Multitasking is a myth—you're really just managing distraction if you're trying to do two things at once. If you're distracted, listeners will detect it.

  If you live with others, I advise placing a sign on your door so that loved ones know to stay out during your interview. My sign reads: *If you're bleeding from the eyes, experiencing chest pain, or holding a winning lottery ticket, come in quietly. If not, go away until I'm off the phone.* Just a suggestion.

- **Use notes, but don't read aloud.** If you're being interviewed remotely, you might be tempted to read prepared answers aloud. In a word—don't. Unless you've got the skills of Meryl Streep, people can tell when you're reading. It gives the impression of coldness or insecurity. A few bullet-list style notes, or your Story Map, are plenty. Trust yourself. Have a chat. Listeners love to feel as though they're eavesdropping on a real conversation, not hearing a prepared spiel.

- **Let the host do the selling.** Good hosts will mention your name and the name of your book at the beginning, the end, and perhaps before and after breaks during your interview. Don't come off like a huckster, pushing people to buy your book. Get them fascinated about the story and its author instead.
- **Prepare to roll with it.** As much as I urge you to prepare yourself and some content for an interview, you may use only part of it, or none at all. Your host or a listener could ask questions that may take you in an entirely different direction than you anticipated. Trust yourself—you've been talking your whole life! Have fun. Enjoy it. If you do, the listeners will too.
- **Be a good sport.** Some shows have playful rituals, little games they like to play with guests. If you've listened to the program, you'll know this. Don't go on if you don't want to play along.

You might also need to be a good sport when it comes to your host. Some are more skilled than others. They could mispronounce your name or say your book title incorrectly. Have a good sense of humor about it. My name is a mouthful. Nearly every host fouls it up. I've learned to laugh and say, *Nice try. I know my name is no bargain.* Then the host often asks me to say it correctly. No big deal. If you get uptight about the small things in an interview, you'll likely miss out on the fun and the opportunity that each interview offers.

Adapt Your Story Map as Interview Prep

Once you've made a Story Map or two (yes, you'll have several versions customized for different audiences) about the topics of your book or your writing, you'll have a solid idea of the kinds of themes you want to focus on and you'll have developed a few stories and other Spellbinders that support the message or messages you want to convey. Though you won't be able to deliver an entire talk in an interview—it's a conversation, not a speech—having your Setup, Chapters, and a few Spellbinders in your back pocket will help you navigate many, if not most, of the questions you'll face.

Even if you never deliver your Story Map as a prepared talk, or if your media interview precedes any live talks you're giving, I suggest working one up as preparation for interviews and even casual conversations. This preparation will give you a well of answers to draw from during an interview or panel discussion. When I'm in an interview, the last thing I want to feel is unprepared and caught off guard. I can't control everything, but I can prepare.

Using Notes

If I'm doing an interview by phone, I'll often have my Story Map in front of me as notes to remind me of the content. If I'm going into a studio, I likely don't use notes at all, but I review them before I go into the studio.

Prepare for the Heat

Just as in any profession, interviewers come in a variety of styles and varying levels of skill. The more controversial the topic of your writing in whatever genre, the more likely you'll experience a more interrogative style of interview. But even if you've written a book about how to train puppies, know this: *The media is a heat-seeking missile.*

Yes, that was an intentionally incendiary Spellbinder I just used. Here's what I mean.

Interviewers seek the "heat" —the passion, the conflict, or the controversy— in every interview. That's what's interesting to listeners. In interviews on controversial topics, they're seeking sensational details, conflict, secrets, sensitive topics, and other "hot" tidbits. If you've written a memoir, they'll likely ask about the most painful or challenging moments, or for behind-the-book details that you may or may not want to talk about. If you've written that puppy training book, they'll gravitate toward information, but also the "warm" *aww* moments and stories. They'll share the story of their old dog that just died or the one that bit them. They want it hot, they want it warm, and they naturally aim for the soft spots. If you've written a novel, they'll likely ask if any of it is based on your real life. They want the heat, the controversy, the emotionally intense information. That's their job.

Be a good interviewee. Bring some heat. Whether your Spellbinders are "hot" controversy, or "warm" emotional moments, don't be a just-the-facts interview. It's a bore. Avoid giving one-word or yes/no answers. Elaborate.

Of course, bring only what's true and don't say more than you choose to say. Use the LEAD technique to field challenging questions, and feel free to link your answers to what you'd like to contribute as you add more detail. The more controversial or sensitive your book, the more prepared you should be to handle aggressive questioning.

It's a Conversation, Not a Soliloquy

Though I encouraged you to elaborate, I don't mean to say that you should deliver a sermon. Remember, your interviewer isn't there just to ask questions. He has a show and a following. His listeners care what he thinks and what his reactions to your ideas might be. Leave room for your interviewer to speak up. You might even ask him a question or two if the conversation lends itself to this.

Prepare for an Unprepared or Newbie Interviewer

I'm a person who prepares for interviews. I listen to other interviews by that host. I research their writing and discover their interests and biases. Still, the question that caught me most off guard was from a radio show host who opened our talk with, *So, what would you like to talk about today?*

I'll admit that I had to use a couple seconds of silence to reorganize my thoughts, and I'm glad I did. What I ended up doing was answering her question with a slightly modified version of the Setup that I'd prepared for my book's launch. I knew it well. It took only about one minute to deliver. I could speak it in a relaxed, conversational way because I'd practiced and delivered it before. It reflected my style, my goal, and what I believe is most important about my story. It was *my* message. By having prepared and delivered this content before, it was available to me. It sounded natural, spontaneous, and conversational.

Using your own Setup to kick things off is also a way to guide less experienced or less skilled interviewers toward the questions that are in your wheelhouse and that you'd like to talk about.

Not every host will turn over control at the start of the whole interview, but many do at the end. Toward the end, I occasionally hear the question, *Is there anything else you wanted to talk about?* Maybe the interviewer ran out of questions before she ran out of time. Or perhaps she simply, graciously, wants to give her guest a chance to include her own thoughts. I like to have a few closing thoughts prepared, just in case.

In any case, it's good to have a few prepared ideas, examples, or stories ready should your host toss control to you.

What If They Ask Something You Don't Want to Answer?

Occasionally an interviewer will ask a question that is either inappropriate or that you just don't want to answer either because it betrays a confidence, it touches on private material, would be embarrassing to someone else, or is not relevant to the topic. Don't pretend you didn't hear the question. Don't evade it and pretend you answered when you didn't. Authenticity matters everywhere, including in interviews.

If this happens, it's important to remember three things:

- If you write a book, you're going to create curiosity so people are going to ask questions and try to uncover secrets.
- You're entitled to have boundaries and don't have to divulge anything you don't want to.
- You do, nonetheless, want to be open, vulnerable, and candid, and provide an interesting interview that puts you in a good light.

Knowing the LEAD technique is a huge advantage here. Rather than reacting harshly, or sounding as though you're either defensive or scolding to your host, **L**isten, then **E**mpathize before you decline to answer, and don't stop there.

Here's an example of how to answer a question you don't want to answer *after* you've listened well to the question:

Empathize: *I get that question a lot and it's perfectly natural to want to know more about that.*

Answer: *I'm not at liberty to answer it specifically because _____. Or Despite how open I am about all that I write about, I do reserve the right to keep some matters private either for myself or on behalf of others. I'm sure you understand.*

Add Detail: *What I can tell you is this: _____.* (This is especially helpful if you provide a Spellbinder here.)

When you add detail, give something juicy, interesting, funny, or colorful. They won't mind if you don't answer as long as you're candid about it, and don't pretend to answer when you're really just pounding your prepared talking points. Politicians do this to such an annoying level that it makes listeners (and interviewers) want to scream. That doesn't mean they won't try to frame the same question another way. Just use the LEAD technique with different content as many times as you need to.

If you're asked something you don't want to talk about, something you don't know, something that would harm someone else if you talked about it, or something that would get you sued, I have one word for you: *don't.* Don't be bullied or tricked or seduced into answering. You can LEAD the Q&A, be polite and respectful to your host, and respect your own privacy and personal ethics. You can give a great interview even if you choose not to answer some questions. The trick is not to be defensive. It's reasonable for people to be curious. Take a breath. Take a beat. Don't take it personally.

Conclusion to Part 4

In part 4, I addressed converting a presentation to a conversation by making room for interaction. To say "it's a conversation" does not mean that you cede your role as presenter. Rather, you make room for the verbal and nonverbal involvement of listeners and use the LEAD model for answering challenging questions in a presentation as well as from media interviewers. To make the most of interview opportunities, I suggest putting in some prep time and taking advantage of the Make It Stick suggestions below.

Interviews, along with interaction during public talks, are a great opportunity to get your ideas and your writing to a wider audience. With a little preparation and some practice, these opportunities can be an important aspect of book promotion and great exposure for you and your books. They can also be great fun.

Make It Stick

Below are suggestions for interviews to either watch or listen to. Some are high-budget productions, others indies. It's useful to watch and listen to interviews to get ideas about what works well for the authors interviewed. Notice that the tone and topics of the interviews can range from serious to playful, as determined by both the subject matter and the program.

EXERCISE #1: LISTEN/LOOK

Listening to authors talk about their stories, their craft, and their views on the world is among my favorite pastimes. YouTube, on-demand television, and podcasts provide a myriad of interviews, from super-famous shows with skilled hosts interviewing bestselling authors to indie podcasters interviewing indie authors, poets, and new voices in the book world.

Do an Internet search for your favorite author. Whether it's a video on YouTube or a link to a podcast, you'll likely find all kinds of opportunities to listen. From living legends to authors long passed, these interviews are a treasure, preserving moments and ideas from those who embody our shared art. Here are just a few:

- **TV:** *Super Soul Sunday*, **host Oprah Winfrey.** Available both on-demand and on the OWN Network website, these slow-paced, thoughtful interviews have a focus on spirituality. Many of the guests are authors. A few of my favorites include: Mark Nepo, Eckhart Tolle, Elizabeth Gilbert, Cheryl Strayed, Norman Lear, and Anne LaMott.
- **Radio:** *Fresh Air*, **host Terry Gross.** Gross is a master interviewer on a wide range of social, entertainment, and political topics. Many of her shows feature authors. You can go to the NPR website and find archived interviews of authors that interest you or download them as podcasts. Two interviews I'd like to draw attention to:
  - **Sherman Alexie** gives an especially heartfelt (and sometimes heartbreaking) interview about his memoir, *You Don't Have to Say You Love Me*. In it, he does

what I love best in an author interview—he lets listeners get to know the person behind the pages and the story behind the story.

○ **Greta Gerwig** is an actor/writer/director. Her *Fresh Air* interview is about writing and directing her film *Ladybird*.

Gross is among the most polite interviewers. With her genuine curiosity and interest, she has a way of luring her guests into revealing things and talking about tender topics, rather than doing so with an aggressive "gotcha" style. I cite the Gerwig interview because it's one in which Gross asks the author something she clearly does not want to talk about, a very tender and controversial topic about a director she worked with in the past. Gerwig chose not to answer those questions. Some admired her for this, others took strong objection. See what you think about how she handled it.

 EXERCISE #2: PODCASTS

- **Ten Minute Writer's Workshop.** As its name implies, these are super-short interviews with authors with a focus on the craft and process of writing. Each one is a treat. I've discovered new authors here as well as heard some of my favorites offer advice. I always have pen and paper handy—there are lots of diamonds in there. This program ended in January of 2018, but the archived episodes remain available.
- **The Newbie Writers Podcast** hosted by Damien Bloth and Catherine Bramkamp. This is a fun show because it focuses on new authors. It also means that you don't have to be famous to get onto the show. (They've kindly welcomed me twice to talk about my first two books.) The format is highly playful. Catherine Bramkamp is a multiply published author who asks most of the "writerly" questions. Damien Bloth is an Australian who serves similarly to the "color man" in sports casting. He comes in with the sometimes silly, sometimes tangential, but always fun comments and questions.

    You'll likely hear a few less polished interviews on this show because these are newbie authors and some may have little experience. That's okay. They're still fun to listen to and offer not only exposure for the author, but information for the listeners. Another freebie and worth a listen.
- **The National Association of Memoir Writers (NAMW),** hosted by NAMW founder, Linda Joy Myers. Though not technically a podcast, NAMW is a fabulous online resource for memoirists and fiction writers alike. You can get the NAMW newsletter for free and learn of the many free webinars and author interviews,

including a massive archive. For a nominal yearly membership, you get more free teleseminars and discounts on additional webinars and resources. Linda Joy Myers is a gentle interviewer who helps her guests shine. A terrific resource.

EXERCISE #3: A TACKY TV RESOURCE

While the show itself is of questionable value (read sometimes tacky) depending upon your taste, the TV show *Shark Tank* offers an opportunity to watch a completely different kind of presentation/interview. The presenters are not authors. They are inventors who are pitching their products to potential investors in a simultaneously artificial and very real setup.

From the serious products to the downright absurd, from skilled presenters to the corniest possible presentation, there's something to learn (good and bad) about the range of presentation styles and the skill level of the pitches. It's informative to watch how the presenters manage very aggressive Q&A from the "sharks." Some of the aggressiveness is for TV (every story needs conflict), but some of it is legitimate. The "sharks" are putting up their own money and they deserve real answers to their questions if they're going to pony up.

- See if you recognize any of the elements of the Story Map in these presentations.
- Look for well-constructed stories and poorly constructed ones.
- Consider which elements of the Story Map you would use to improve the weaker presentations.
- Observe to see if the guests LEAD the interaction. This is where the presentation often turns toward success or disaster.
- Take note of the delivery skills and visuals that the presenters use. What works? What doesn't? What makes a pitch sophisticated? What makes it tacky (beyond the products themselves)? Pinpoint the content and the delivery skills that tilt a presentation toward tacky or sophisticated.

Though I'd never recommend *Shark Tank* as deep or inspiring viewing, I believe that opportunities to learn about writing and speaking come from all kinds of places. Films, TV talk shows, movies, commercials, even in your house of worship.

Have a notepad at the ready. Opportunities to learn good storytelling skills are everywhere!

PART 5

Add the Bling: Touches That

Make a Talk Memorable

"It is a happy talent to know how to play."
—Ralph Waldo Emerson

In the Invitation and parts 1–4 of this book, I addressed the essential elements of WHY to speak, WHAT to say, and HOW to use solid delivery skills to speak with skill and confidence both as the speaker and in managing interaction with listeners. Now that you have an organized, well-crafted story and natural, confident delivery skills, you have a solid enough structure for your talk that you can afford to play a bit. Add some bling. Make it fun, memorable, poignant.

In part 5, we'll switch things up a bit in both style and content. The chapters in this section are about the extras that can make a speaking event more memorable. Once you have the core elements of public speaking addressed in the earlier parts of this book down, it will be the extras—the bling—that can make an event a delight for the speaker and the listeners. These chapters are in the form of fattened-up lists for easy access.

In part 5 we'll cover:

- Tips on using visual support during talks
- Readings that work: Selecting and delivering written content
- How to be a skilled event host, panel moderator, or emcee
- The extra extras: Food, giveaways, and more
- Tips for pitches and parties

CHAPTER 20

The Eyes Have It:
Make Great Use of Visual Support

A large percentage of the space in the human brain is devoted to receiving, interpreting, and storing visual images. Space in your audience members' minds and memories is valuable real estate. Lasting memories are beachfront property! Using visuals to help listeners understand, interpret, or retain your content can help you stake claim to some of that invaluable mental space.

Does Your Topic Lend Itself to Visual Support?

As writers, not all of our speaking events lend themselves to the use of visual aids such as slides and flip charts. Book launches, readings, and panels rarely include them. Other speaking events lend themselves more to visuals: workshops, classes, keynote addresses, TED Talks, and so on. Whenever we use visuals, it's important to remember that nobody comes to an author event because they're excited to see your slide deck and handouts. Make use of visuals to support you but remember, they're not the main event—you and your story are the stars.

Visuals, designed well and used well, can captivate audiences and gain memorability for your story and your ideas. Designed poorly, or delivered poorly, visual aids compete with you for your listeners' highly prized mental real estate. Bumbling with poor visuals will crowd out any positives that can be gained by including them. Visuals that occupy too much of the speaker's focus or cause distraction keep her from telling her story and connecting to her listeners.

This chapter provides a list of general guidelines to help you make use of visuals of various kinds at writer/author events. Whether you're using presentation software (PowerPoint, for example), a flip chart or whiteboard, a handout, a prop, or a demo, remember this: Your story is what's most important. The visuals are only there to help. If they don't help, better to leave them out.

Guidelines for Using Visuals Effectively

Story first, visuals after
It is my strong suggestion— if you're choosing to add visuals (slides, handouts, props, and so on) to your talk—that you design the Story Map (your message) *before* you design the slides. Visuals are simply one type of Spellbinder to help you communicate your story. Slides are not your story.

Simplify
Visuals that are cluttered, busy, or too detailed are a distraction rather than an aid to speakers. They become your competition for audience. Don't use fifteen fonts and twenty colors.

Beautify
Simple text slides, charts, and handouts are the easiest ones to make, but the old bulleted lists do not make for visually compelling additions to a talk. A near-infinite supply of photography and graphics is available on the Internet for free or for a small fee. Presentation software tutorials are available for free on YouTube. Get a little creative with your slides. It's an old cliché, but true nonetheless: a picture really is worth a thousand words.

Limit the number of visuals
Unless you're an art historian or photojournalist where the slides are an essential element of your talk, you don't want to devote much of your time to visuals. For most of us, the visuals are the bling, not the content. For a short workshop, I try to keep visuals to three or four slides (or fewer) for each ten to fifteen minutes of teaching time. For a workshop of several hours or all day, the ratio changes. Three slides every ten minutes for the whole day would be a barrage of slides! You don't want to make people feel like they're stuck watching a slide show.

Avoid offering an eye chart
If you're using visuals, make sure they're visible and legible to the whole group. If you have to say, *I know you can't see this but . . .*, it's not a well-designed visual. Font size should be big enough to read from a distance; details in an image or chart (if they're small) should be blown up to a size visible in the cheap seats.

Resist using your visuals as your speaker notes

Some speakers pack all their information onto their slides or charts to remind them of their own content. This clutters your visuals and encourages a host of bad habits. Design your content. Make a simple, one-page map of your notes (the Story Map discussed earlier) and reserve visuals as Spellbinders that you add to your talk.

Talk to people, not projections

It's tempting to look at your slides or charts and to read them or talk toward them. If you've disregarded the suggestion just before this one and are reading the slides as your notes, you're more likely to talk toward your slide while reading. Remember my one and only unbreakable delivery skill rule? *You only get to talk to people.*

Don't talk while you write

If you're writing as part of a workshop—either drawing a concept or capturing audience ideas and writing them—don't try to talk while you write. It'll make your handwriting a illegible, and you'll be breaking that one and only rule again. Use silence while you write. Write only a bit at a time. Prewrite charts and longer quotes beforehand, if you can.

Let them see it!

You don't want your visuals to be like bad subtitles that go by so fast your audience can't read them. If they're important enough to use, they're important enough to let the audience see and absorb them. Just like every other element of your talk, *Don't talk during their movie.* Reveal your slide or your chart, then use silence to let your listeners look at, read, and absorb a visual when you reveal it. *Shhhhh.* Be silent while they do. You can check your notes, look at the visual for reminders, or just think through your next point while they're looking at the visual you've provided. After they've absorbed it, they'll look back to you. This is your indicator that their show is over and they're ready to hear from you again.

Have a backup plan

Here's a shocker: technology fails. Often. If your talk is highly dependent upon visual support, have a backup plan. Bring slides on a flash drive to use on a borrowed computer if yours crashes. Create a printout of slides (I print them as handouts with six or eight slides to a page) that can be quickly copied, turning your slides into handouts. Using a chart or whiteboard can replace some technological visuals as a backup. In any case, remember you have a story to tell that is valuable with or without visuals.

Don't let visuals boss you around

Too many speakers get derailed by their own visuals. They spend hours designing them, freak out if the technology fails, and essentially let the visuals boss them around. Resist giving visuals any more importance or power than they're due. If they flop, laugh it off and move on. Your story, your message, and you are far more important than a slide or a handout.

Bring the right hardware

I have a small bag that I insert in my tote whenever I'm using technology for a presentation. I have several different adapters and an extension cord. It's possible that the hotel, bookstore, or conference hall will have equipment that needs a special adapter, and equipment is evolving all the time. Find out as much as you can ahead of time and be prepared. I label all my equipment with a colorful tag and my name and number on it so that I don't lose items.

Use a remote

If I'm using slides and not presenting in a seated meeting where my laptop is right next to me, I prefer to advance slides with a remote rather than being tied to my laptop. This gives me freedom to move around the room. Remotes are available at various price ranges from modest to ridiculous. Frankly, simple ones are better. Do resist fiddling with your remote as a nervous gesture. Set it down when not in use.

Don't be an accidental copyright criminal

Just because you can download it doesn't mean you own the rights to it. Photographs, cartoons, charts, graphs, and other visual materials (as well as video clips and music) are often copyrighted material that you have to obtain permission, and sometimes pay a licensing fee, to use. I met a speaker who used a cartoon that he'd clipped from his newspaper in a slide show for his talk at a conference and received a ten-thousand-dollar fine for not having obtained permission. Another presenter brought music CDs and used them during a conference workshop. She was fined for using that music without permission. (There are scouts at conferences looking for such violations.) Without intending to do so, both these folks broke copyright laws. You're promoting your work when you speak and that's a commercial venture. That means you are not entitled to use images, clips, music, and so on for which you've not obtained permission. It's different in an academic or nonprofit setting where, if credited properly, many visuals are available without permissions. It's always worth it to check. Fines can be hefty and the originators deserve credit for their work.

Avoid cheesy clip art

A whole host of Internet sites are available for downloading free or purchasable art to add to your slides and printed visuals. Using the canned clip art in PowerPoint or other presentation software cheapens a presentation rather than adding to it.

Choose only visuals that add to your story

If a visual doesn't support your POV or amplify one of the points that does, it doesn't belong in your presentation. Don't add visuals just to be cute. Visuals should be relevant. Just because it's cute doesn't mean it belongs in your story.

Use images to increase emotional intensity

Whether offering a visual image that shows tragic circumstances relevant to your talk, or using a silly cat photo to add relevant humor to your talk, visual material can increase the emotional intensity of a presentation. They can be used for drama, impact, humor, or clarity; see how you might use images to touch hearts and tickle funny bones.

Consider color for handouts you make yourself

If I print programs for a live event or offer a simple handout, I'll often print it on brightly colored paper and have it on the seats before audience walks in. The color is eye-catching and I don't have to fuss with handing them out later. A program with the list of readers and the host's contact information is a nice touch. White paper tends to disappear.

Remember that you are the best visual in the room

Gestures, facial expressions, and body posture can be used for visual interest and can have a far bigger impact than any computer-generated image.

A handout I recommend for authors

Many of our non-writer friends and audience members are ever so happy to support us as authors. They're excited to buy our books and attend our events. Despite their desire to do so, often they don't know how to support you beyond buying your book. I have a handout that I print for every author talk I give. It includes tips on how to support indie authors and includes info on writing reviews, requesting that their local libraries stock your book, making your book a selection for book clubs, and so forth. I tuck one of these lists into every book I sell or give away and place one on every seat for my events. It also has my contact information. Help people help you and your book.

Don't let your visuals distract you from your main purpose

I've worked with many speakers who pull all-nighters creating and tweaking their visuals the night before a big presentation. The next day they're wrung out. Their visuals are terrific, but they're not at their best for delivering their talk. Keep perspective about what's important. The bulk of your time should be designing and practicing your talk. The visuals are the bling, not the substance.

You can pause your visuals, too!

Here's a nifty trick if you're using PowerPoint or other computer generated visuals. If you want to refocus your listeners' attention back onto yourself and away from a slide from which you've moved on, you can do so by simply going to black. To do this, you can either press the B key on your computer keyboard, or find the blackout button on the remote you're using to advance slides. When you're moving onto a new topic, coming to the close of your talk, or otherwise want to refocus the attention of your listeners, going to black is a great technique.

Make it personal

Using your own photographs and art, or choosing images that mean something to you personally, adds a dimension to the value of using visuals. This is way better than canned clip art. To "illustrate" my point about making a talk personal, here's a photo I often use at the end of a talk on my "Thank you" slide. This is a pic of my sweet writing companion, Edgar Allan Paw.

Much of the human brain is devoted to taking in, interpreting, and storing visual memory. Visuals don't replace your content or your story. Be sure your visuals are your aids, not your competitors. Chosen carefully and used well, visuals can add a dynamic Spellbinder to a presentation.

The big take-away here is to let your visuals aid your story, not replace it. Your story and your connection to your listeners is what matters most. The rest, well, it's just bling.

CHAPTER 21

Virtual Presentations:

The Next Best Thing to Being There

~⁔~

Once upon a time video conferencing and virtual presentations didn't exist except on "The Jetsons". (Younger readers can ask their parents and grandparents about how we all survived these primitive times.)

Today we have an ever-increasing number of platforms for connecting with others via technology. These technologies offer writers another set of both opportunities and challenges for increasing their visibility, reaching a wider audience, and making connections to others without ever boarding a plane or packing a bag. We can teach classes, deliver talks, meet with our writing support groups, and attend virtual book clubs, all while wearing our fuzzy slippers. Attending book club meetings thousands of miles from my house by using video-telecom technology is great fun, meeting with readers, and talking with book lovers whom I'd otherwise never have had a chance to meet.

Unfortunately, the advantages of presenting virtually turn into disadvantages if we fail to adapt our public speaking skills for these alternative portals of communication. Virtual presentations can feel hollow and impersonal to viewers. Speakers can be distracted by—or worse, overwhelmed by—the technological challenges of the platforms they're using. Audiences can be less engaged because they're dealing with a host of additional distractions, some in their listening environment, and others because of the mechanics of the technology itself. Rather than being "storytellers", we can appear as very ignorable talking heads.

What we want in any virtual presentation is the same thing we want in an in-person one: to bridge the divide between ourselves, and our listeners, and to engage audience members in a personal way.

The fundamental skills throughout this book are equally applicable to virtual presentations, with minor modifications to bring warmth and to "humanize" a presentation and to adapt to any technological platform. With a few adjustments to your skills, your virtual presentations can help you to forge powerful and personal connections to listeners just as they do when your listeners are in the room with you.

Whether you're a technology whiz or a technophobe, I invite you to embrace the possibility of communicating via virtual presentations. Some virtual presentations are slick, with high production values, while others—the ones most of us writers will use—are simpler, and doable if you have some basic skills and a smart phone. It all depends on your goals.

What I offer here is not a tech class on the mechanics of how to use each kind of virtual platform. Those skills are better learned in classes devoted to the application you want to use and can either be gained by attending a class, watching online videos, or having a tech-savvy friend help you out. Here, I offer a fattened-up list of principles and techniques that enhance your delivery skills for use across all platforms, be they conference calls that can include a few or hundreds of listeners, video conversations using applications such as Skype and Zoom, or webinars delivered through a computer screen.

General Tips for All Virtual Presentations

While there are dozens of variations, platforms, and apps to facilitate each of these media options, the general principles and techniques I offer below will cross all of them.

Shorter is better. Attention span for listening during a virtual presentation is shortened in any virtual presentation. Nobody can pay full attention for a three-hour conference call. With rare exception, an hour is about maximum for most virtual presentations if you want to maintain audience attention and engagement. For Facebook Live events and other "announcement" kind of presentations, just a few minutes will do. TED Talks are under eighteen minutes for a reason!

Energy is vital. When presenting in a virtual environment, unable to see the faces of listeners, it's easy to let your own energy go flat. Even when an audience cannot see me, I wear a portable headset and I stand, gesture, and move about the room as if my audience is right there with me. While listeners may not be able to see what I'm doing, my behaviors inform and energize my voice. This radically changes the vocal quality for the better.

Posture is important, even if they can't see you. Obviously, posture—or what I call Stance—is important when people can see you. It's equally important when they can't. When speakers deliver an audio-only presentation, say, a conference call, they're tempted to sit, to slouch, and to keep their chins down while they're reading their notes. All of these serve to dampen the resonance in the speaker's voice, making it sound lifeless. Even if they can't see you, sit or stand straight, raise your chin. Animate your voice.

Don't forget the value of silence. When we're alone in our home offices, delivering a talk via technology, it's easy to fly through the content without pausing at all. But remember, it's during silence that engagement happens and it's those pauses that will help you to eliminate those weedy non-words. In an audio only call, those ums and ers, lip smacks, and y'knows will stand out even more than in a live talk. Apply the same principles of pausing that I talked about in part 3. They're even more crucial in virtual presentations.

Minimize distractions. Our home and workplace environments can be distracting places. This is true for both presenters and listeners. Of course, we can't control for every variable. (It seems that my neighbor gets inspired to use his leaf blower as soon as I start a webinar.) But we *can* control the controllables. Make sure your phone's ringer is silenced. Even a vibrating cell phone on a desk will be loud to your listeners, and distracting to you. See that noisy pets are either in another part of the house or cared for elsewhere. Don't wear jangly jewelry that makes distracting sounds. Have tissues, a glass of water, and a throat lozenge handy. Sniffing and throat clearing are excruciatingly loud on a conference call. Cover the microphone if you need to sneeze, cough, or clear your throat. Put a sign on your door to keep family members or roommates from interrupting, and a sign on the front door that says, "Please do not knock or ring the bell." In short, make sure that your space is quiet and that the probability of noisy interruptions is reduced.

Prepare, times five. When you're delivering a talk in a virtual environment, you have to prepare and practice your content as you would for any presentation. Your Story Map will work perfectly here for organizing content. In a virtual environment you'll also need to practice with whatever technology you're using as well. I strongly advise doing several practice runs with new technology. Get a pal or a loved one to do a mock class with you, whether it's a simple conference call or a video. You'll want to discover and work out all of the bugs before the real presentation.

Resist reading a script. It's already hard enough to engage listeners in a virtual format. Reading a script can make it feel as though the speaker is even more remote than if she's speaking in a more conversational way. Unless you're using a virtual format specifically for a read-aloud opportunity, it's better to be conversational. Again, a Story Map can help.

Spellbinders are more important than ever! Let's face it—video classes and tele-seminars run the risk of being bo-ring! Information is hard enough to absorb when you're listening in person. In a virtual class, it can be deadly. Lots of presenters get very flat and serious during virtual presentations. I think it's because they can't see listeners and it kills their energy a bit. By remembering to use lively Spellbinders—stories, analogies, humor, and such—it will energize your talk and cause your listeners to "prairie dog"—pop their little heads up in attention—even if you can't see them do it. Have some fun. Get creative. It's good for you and your listeners.

Mute the line if you can. The single biggest annoyance (besides tech glitches) on conference calls is when you have a listener with a noisy environment. From barking dogs to shuffling papers, the distractions in home environments can range from irritating to deafening. (I've even heard toilets flush during conference calls. EEK!) I always do a bit of housekeeping at the top of a call, letting listeners know that I'll be muting the line, only "un-muting" it when I'm opening up for questions.

Make room for your listeners. If you're delivering content during a conference call or a webinar and people are listening live (as opposed to in a recording) I suggest making room for them to ask questions or make comments if it's at all possible with your technology. If you have many listeners on the line, having them interrupt at will for their questions can be too disruptive. Instead, I build in several "park benches", or stopping points right into my Story Map. When I deliver the agenda—here called the Itinerary—I let listeners know that I'll stop twice during the talk, and that there will be room at the end for them to ask questions. Some platforms allow people to write questions and comments into a chat space that you can scan during those stops. With smaller groups on conference calls you can invite listeners to speak their questions.

Some webinar programs allow for nonverbal interaction: raising of hands, circling items, voting, and more. If used well, these can increase interaction. I'm a bit cautious about them being overused and getting corny and gimmicky, but it's worth experimenting to see if you can use them in a fun, interactive, and authentic way.

Use the buddy system. If you're conducting classes, delivering a series, or facilitating a regular group via webinar or conference call, it's great if you can have a partner who can monitor and troubleshoot technology problems and participant interaction. He can monitor the chat for complications—sound problems, loss of connections, distracting noises, and so forth—and let you know. Freed of having to focus on this stuff, you can instead focus on your presentation. Some platforms—the pricy ones—come with on-call tech support. Others, you're more on your own.

Roll with the tech hassles. Even if you've used a technology many times, glitches can happen. Tech screws up; what can I say? The most common glitch is an echo on the line. It's maddening. Though these things can be so frustrating, it's important that the presenter stays cool. Breathe. Convey a brief apology so that you or your facilitator can attempt to fix the problem. If it persists, ask your listeners to curse the technology gods with you and request that they hang up and call in again. This often (though not always) fixes the echo problem. The crucial thing here is to express your frustration with the technology, but to convey warmth and good humor to listeners. If you do, they'll blame the tech gods and not you. A sense of humor about glitches and tech fails goes a long way.

Remember your LEAD techniques for managing challenging questions. I have no science for this, but it's my intuitive feeling that some feistier participants are emboldened in a virtual environments. My experience is that aggressive questioners are a bit braver in virtual classes than during in-person ones. (Timid ones are even more timid and require a bit of prodding to participate.) Perhaps it's the anonymity. In any case, the technique— Listen, Empathize, Answer, and add Detail—is as important here as it is during any kind of presentation.

Book clubs can be a blast. I've had great fun as a virtual guest in book clubs across the country. Skype, and recently, Zoom are the most common applications for this kind of informal gathering. The host on the other end gets a big screen and gathers the group around the table. To add an extra bit of connection, I ask ahead of time about the group's traditions. If they have wine or coffee, I have some on my end. It's like we're sharing a real gathering. It's as the old Bell Telephone ads used to say, "the next best thing to being there."

A Few Specific Tips for Video Presentations

For lots of us, the mere idea of being filmed brings up all kinds of anxiety. I get it; believe me. Our inner critic runs wild with our feelings of self-consciousness about everything from the way we look to the way we talk, and fears of being judged or looking foolish. Time for a quick shift of thinking:

Once we've jumped the mental hurdle, overcoming our hesitancy about being on camera, a few adaptation of our techniques can help us to look, sound, and feel better while we're delivering presentations. Remember, this is a way to reach an audience that you might otherwise never reach. Learning to present your ideas in via filmed media is an invaluable skill and can be a vital part of an author's platform.

Think of the camera's lens as the eyes of your entire audience. If you are a lone presenter, talking to your viewing audience from your writing room, remember this: to look into the camera's lens is to make eye contact with your viewers. This is a tricky one, I'll admit, especially for those of us who have not trained as broadcasters. If you have a PowerPoint slide show, or notes, or some other technology feature that captures your attention, every time you look at those things on your screen you are looking away from the eyes of your listeners. While you don't have to stare into the lens of your computer or smart phone continuously, you must look at it for much of the time that you're speaking to your viewers or they'll get the impression that you're distracted or spacy. This is eye contact. Remember my rule: Speak only to people. This is true, even if your "people" are not in the room with you.

It's especially challenging to look into the lens when your screen also has a segment devoted to your own projected image, as some teleconference platforms do. If you look down at yourself, your virtual audience will see you speaking, but you'll be looking off into the distance, from their vantage. This can be distancing to your viewers.

In order to remind myself to look into the lens I have a giant "smile" mask taped near my desktop computer's camera lens. You can go to your local crafts supply store and get a silly pair of googly eyes (usually used for plush toys) and affix them on either side of your computer's camera lens. These all serve to remind you to talk to your listeners, making eye contact with the lens and they're silly enough to remind you to smile. Anything that helps you remember to look into the lens is fine by me.

Move. I'm amazed how many people freeze as soon as a video camera is on. It's not still photography. Remember to animate yourself—face, body, and voice—for visual variety. Walking around may not look natural, of course, if you're presenting via your computer's camera without an audience present, but using your arms to gesture, varying your facial expression, and employing all of the musical elements of your voice in an engaging way make for great TV. Animate!

Dress simply. Of course, if we're broadcasting a video of ourselves, most of us want to look our best. Unless you're a fashion designer wearing the latest avant-garde fashions, I think it's generally wise to keep clothing, simple, tasteful, and not distracting. Your level of dressing up is determined by your personal style and the topic you're talking about. If you've written a book about skateboarding techniques for a teen audience, you certainly wouldn't wear a suit. Dress appropriately to your topic and your audience. For most of us, simple, solid-color clothing works best. It's best to avoid super busy patterns that can distract. If you're speaking about a cause or a movement, you might choose to wear the colors associated with that cause or a t-shirt bearing their logo.

Occasionally, particularly in the case of a book launch or talk about a work of historical fiction, it can be fun to wear clothing from the era of your book. Christie Nelson wrote *Beautiful Illusion,* a fabulous historical novel about San Francisco's Golden Gate International Exposition in 1939. At her launch, she wore a vintage suit and hat, suited to the period of her story. It was quite a Spellbinder, and fun, too.

TIP: Do be cautious about dressing up from the waste up only. I once attended a videoconference where the presenter was dressed in a lovely sweater and an elegant necklace, but when her kitty knocked over a lamp and she popped up to catch it, the whole conference got a glimpse of her pajama bottoms covered with Curious George images. Glad she was wearing jammies.

Tidy up, but not too much. If you're presenting via video from your home office, it's good to survey your surroundings. Be sure you don't have a reflective surface behind you, that you have plenty of light, and that your environment is clear of extreme distractions. Of course, I tidy up the visible parts of my office a bit when I'm on camera for a presentation. Still, your environment shouldn't be too sterile. It should look personal. I love seeing a writer's studio, a bit of her décor, even a well-stocked bookshelf behind her. If it's too much of a mess, though, I'm looking more at the contents of the office than I am listening to the content. Keep it personal, but not distracting.

Nobody wants to look up your nose. If you're using your computer's camera or your smart phone to film your presentations, it's unflattering to film from below your chin. Nobody looks great from that angle. Use a tripod, stack some books, or do something to raise the angle of whatever device you're using to film your presentation. It's a more flattering angle and you don't reveal your nostrils to the world..

It's not the Blair Witch Project. In 1999 a little indie film exploded in popularity in the U.S. The "Blair Witch Project" had a low-tech, shaky camera effect that made it appear that it was homemade documentation of a real life, paranormal event, when really it was indie filmmakers making it appear as such. It was the "shaky camera" filming that gave the movie an eerie, homemade feel and the verisimilitude of a truly haunting encounter.

This shaky camera thing was fun for this groundbreaking movie, but not so fun for your own video presentations. If you're using a smart phone or a hand-held mini-camera to film your presentations, I advise using a tripod or some other way to stabilize your device. The shaky camera effect gets annoying—and in extreme cases, even a little nauseating—for audiences. I got a tripod for my iPhone at Target for about ten bucks. This is far superior to trying to hold a camera "selfie style". It doesn't have to be fancy or expensive.

It's not all about slick production values. But for that shaky camera effect I mentioned, it's important to know that not all of our video presentations require expensive high production values. A simple video of your excitement when you're opening the box containing your brand new baby books can be a great social media moment.

I mentioned Martha Alderson, the author of *The Plot Whisperer* in an earlier chapter. Alderson offers a plot workshop in a series of short low-tech videos. She is outdoors where the light is beautiful and she gives casual talks, each just a few minutes in length. The wind blows her hair a bit, but she is clearly at home, comfortable, and happy in her setting. It's not high production, but her videos are of high value.

The worlds of social media and virtual presentations can feel overwhelming. I take a "baby steps" approach to learning and using these ever-growing opportunities and technologies. I can't learn about them all at once, so I watch the exploits of my community of writers, learn from them, swap information, and try a bit at a time. Most importantly, I never forget that the technology is merely a vehicle for connecting to a wider audience of real people, and that the same authenticity and simple skills I use during in-person connections are much the same during virtual ones.

I invite you to observe all kinds of virtual presentations: conference calls, webinars, Zoom meetings, Facebook Live events, and others. Just as suggested in all of the Make It Stick exercises throughout this book, take note. Notice what you like and what you don't, what works best, and what gets in your way of your having the most positive experience during a virtual meeting, class, or event. By developing a few extra skills and applying the ones I've taught throughout this book, you'll be able to use whatever format you choose and to do so with skill and confidence.

Just remember to have a bit of fun.

CHAPTER 22

Readings That Work

*"You don't have to be an actor or an extrovert to give a fine reading.
It's not about grandstanding—it's about sending your words floating out into
the air where listeners can breathe them in and feel them open up inside."*
—Gabriel Cohen, author and renowned reading-series host

Reading our work to listeners is one of the most common public speaking experiences for writers. It's worth a chapter to look at how to choose and deliver your reading selections.

One of the best things I ever did for my own development as a writer and as a speaker has been to host (and sometimes cohost) a reading series that featured other writers. In doing so, not only do I get to enjoy a wide range of both prose and poetry, I get to study what works and what doesn't when reading written work aloud to an audience. I learned firsthand—through trial and error at my audience's expense, I'm afraid—what kinds of formats work best and worst when you're a moderator/facilitator/host, and what goes into a great introduction when you're welcoming someone else to the stage. I encourage you to not only take note of the tips in this chapter, but to recognize the value of both reading for and possibly hosting such readings and other events that support your fellow writers. It's a great way to build community, and listening to great stories and poetry is a terrific way to spend a Sunday afternoon or a Saturday night.

Opportunities to read your work include:

- Events devoted to featuring readers, usually called "readers' series," "slams," or "salons"
- As part of a media interview (radio, TV, podcast)
- As part of a panel discussion where readings are invited
- To serve as a Spellbinder, as part of a talk you're giving

Whatever the venue, you'll want to make the most of your reading opportunity. This puts your work (and you) in a good light. Reading dynamically with emotional impact gets you invited back, sometimes by popular demand. This helps your visibility, also known as building your platform.

Readings That Work for You and Your Listeners

Reading your work is a great way to gain exposure for your books, stories, or poems. In his article "A Special Beast," Gabriel Cohen describes the advantages of readings and how to do them well. His suggestions mirror my own experience as a reader, as a host of readers, and as a coach helping other authors choose their read-aloud selections. Of all of his great suggestions, this is the most crucial:

> *"A reading is not about the book; it's about the experience of the reading."*

It's fine, wonderful in fact, that doing a reading serves both the writer and the audience. Most of the poets and writers that have been my guests have offered beautiful experiences to their audiences. The smaller group who did poorly did so for one of two main reasons: they weren't prepared, or they made it all about themselves rather than the listeners. Here are tips to help you get into the vantage of your audience:

The audience is there to be entertained.
They don't need to meet every character, learn the entire plot, or be impressed by your purple prose. If you're reading short works or an excerpt, select pieces that are emotionally engaging, be they dramatic, funny, suspenseful, surprising, or heartwarming.

Works in progress are fine, but polish them up.
Some reading opportunities—open-mike events, for example—lend themselves to reading works in progress. This can be a great opportunity for the writer to get a feel for the impact of her story, but it should not be at the expense of the listeners. Reading selections don't have to be in their final edited state, but should not be in rugged rough-draft form. Whatever you read—even if it's not in its final, final form—should be a cohesive, engaging experience for your listeners. For prestigious readers' series, some of which are recorded and broadcast, as well as for media interviews, it's best to choose a polished selection that is in audience-ready shape. And please, practice the work aloud to prepare.

Limit exposition.

Listening is different than reading silently. I'm a fan of crafted writing and literary fiction and appreciate well-drawn prose. Still, when reading aloud, expository writing and lengthy descriptions tend be less engaging to listeners. Unless you've got mad acting skills that can make reading a phonebook exciting, I recommend selecting a more accessible excerpt.

Scenes work well.

Readings that include action and crisp dialogue are generally better for captivating audiences than lengthy description. Usually a scene with just two or three characters works best for short readings. It's hard for audiences to keep track of a lot of characters they've just met.

Choose emotionally engaging pieces.

Whether it's conflict, suspense, intrigue, or humor, engaging listeners on an emotional level makes a reading dynamic. Appeal to their hearts, their curiosity, or their funny bones and they're in.

Select an excerpt with stand-alone value.

A reading should provide an entertaining experience for listeners, even if they don't read your book. Being entertained is what makes listeners want to read your book.

Shorter is usually better.

Whether you're one of several readers at an event, you're reading an excerpt at your book's launch, or you're reading as part of an interview or panel, your host will likely offer you a time limit. Most salons featuring multiple readers will give you five to ten minutes to read. If you're a singular, featured reader you may get more time, but it's likely better to do two or three short readings rather than one twenty-minute one. When listening, audiences have a more limited attention span than when they're reading. Give them a taste, not a whole feast.

Limit backstory and too much setup.

If you're reading from a section other than the beginning of a book, you might need to set it up for your listeners by mentioning who a character is or what happened just prior to the scene you're reading. If this can be done in thirty seconds or so, that's fine. If it requires much more explanation than that, you might want to choose a different passage. Your backstory is part of your total stage time, so calculate that into your time assessment.

Poets are sometimes the worst offenders here, offering lengthy backstory to each and every poem. A bit of explanation is fine, but your work should speak for itself. By all means, do share brief tidbits of the origin of the story or poem to make it interesting. Brief is key.

Honor time limits.

This is just good manners. It's squirm-worthy for the host, fellow readers, and possibly the audience if one reader grossly exceeds her allotted time at an event featuring multiple readers. The venue may be available for a limited time and the event may be advertised as a certain length. Reading, like speaking, usually takes longer than you think. Practice aloud and time it to see if your selection fits into your time allotment. The last thing a host wants to do is fetch the hook to pull you off stage. She'll likely respond by simply not inviting you back. I would, and I have not invited writers back to my events because they've utterly disregarded time limits, or because they're chronically late. I have a strict "no prima donnas" rule, and have learned that many hosts do, too.

No shuffling!

Whether you're a poet reading multiple pieces or you're reading an excerpt or two from a larger work, have your selections clearly marked and organized. Put your poems into an order rather than deciding on the spot. It's tedious to listeners when readers shuffle through papers or thumb through their book to find a reading. It also gives the impression that you didn't prepare.

When reading a book excerpt, consider printing it rather than reading it from a book. I often enlarge the font and add extra space between lines so that I can read more easily. If you wear reading glasses, wear them. The quality of the reading is more important than vanity.

Alter or rearrange your written work for a livelier reading.

This is another good reason for printing out your copy onto paper rather than reading it from a published book. I mark up my copy. I use a Sharpie to block cut out most of the dialogue attributions (he said, she said, etc.) because when reading aloud, they're often not needed. I cross out lines and paragraphs that slow the action for listeners or that are only relevant to the whole book, rather than just the scene being read. I may write in a word or two for clarification to replace a whole paragraph that I edited out. When I'm done with it, my copy looks like a redacted secret document. That's okay. It's all done with the audience in mind. If you prefer, you can print a cleaner altered copy, of course.

Mix it up.

If you're reading more than one excerpt, story, or poem, I suggest choosing pieces that are varied in tone, from heavy to light. Variety adds interest. Fifteen minutes of elegies can be taxing.

Avoid the bait and switch.

Learn from a mistake I made as a new author. I read two excerpts from my novel that were lighthearted, even funny. Those are legitimate parts of the book and provide contrast to much darker story lines. I had more than one reader (and one who reviewed the book on Amazon) report that they felt "deceived," thinking they were buying a light romance rather than the dark and tragic love story that it is. Make sure that at least one of your selections represents the nature of your book.

Select content appropriate to the event.

When it comes to explicit material, be thoughtful. Strong language, violence, or sexual scenes may be fitting for one venue and wrong for another. If you're reading on the radio, FCC requirements limit the use of some vocabulary. When you're speaking or reading, honor the guidelines or your host or station can be fined.

If you're reading in a public venue such as a library or bookstore where patrons, including children, might wander in unaware, you may choose to limit strong language, select a PG-rated scene, or alter some of the coarser language. Poetry slams and adults-only open-mike events may be a no-holds-barred environment, but not every event is. Ask your host for input about their guidelines.

Don't give away the farm.

I attended one book launch event where the author read so many excerpts of her book that I didn't feel that I needed to buy it. Give a taste, not the meal. And please—no spoilers.

Read something easy for listeners to grasp.

If you have a complex story with dozens of characters and an intricate plot, it may be great reading, but hard to follow as a read-aloud. Select a scene that is simpler, with fewer characters. If you confuse people, they'll likely not be interested in the story.

Get creative!

Now and then it's fun to try something other than "just reading." For example, if you're reading a scene with lots of dialogue between two characters, consider inviting a trusted friend (who is a good reader) to read one of the parts. It'll be like a mini-theater experience for your listeners, and you can delete all of the attributions and much of the description. Or, you could have two readers do the dialogue while you read the narrative. If you do it this way, be sure to mark out all of the tags; "he said" and "she said" can be real clunkers in a dramatic reading.

One drink beforehand is likely plenty.

Many writing events include alcohol and lots of writers find a drink calms their nerves before an event. If that works for you, great, but you want to be relaxed, not sloppy. I've been to more than one poetry slam or reading event where the guest (or worse, the host) imbibed too heavily and crossed from fun to embarrassing. Read first, drink later. 'Nuff said.

Selecting and delivering readings is a frequent part of a writer's public speaking life. It pays to put some thought into how to select and how to deliver what you read. It also pays to develop your "reading chops." Learn to play with the dynamics of your voice. Channel your inner performer. After all, you want people to fall in love with your stories, and when they do, it's glorious.

CHAPTER 23

Be a Skilled Event Host, Panel Moderator, or Emcee

"All things are difficult before they are easy."
—Thomas Fuller, clergyman

As you gain a reputation for being a good speaker—and you will—you may get opportunities to serve as a host, a panel moderator, or to make introductions of other authors at their events. Take them! The more you do this and do it well, the more you'll be asked to do it. In this chapter, we'll cover why you should be a host, and I'll give tips for hosting, events, and making introductions.

Why Bother Hosting When It's Not about Your Own Work?

Here's a long list of answers for you.

- It's a way to enlarge your community of writers.
- It supports the art form and its artists.
- It's another subtle bit of exposure for you and your writing, even if you're not reading your work.
- If you host a regular event, you gather a great mailing list that you can use to promote the event as well as to expand your list for your own promotions. (I always disclose this when I ask people to sign up for the list along with the promise that my emails will be infrequent and that I won't share the list.)
- It's a way to make connections with book professionals and coordinators of writers' conferences. These come in handy when you want to be a part of their events later.

- Being a host rather than a featured speaker gives you a chance to hone your speaking skills with less pressure.
- It's fun! Pure and simple, being part of readings and other writer events is a great way to spend time with your tribe-mates and other word lovers.

Be the Host With the Most!

Acting as host or moderator of an event is another application of public speaking skills. Here are just a few tips for serving this role well. When I host an event, I always keep in mind that I am there for two reasons: to provide an entertaining experience for the audience and to provide a supportive environment for the writers who are sharing their talents to provide that experience. It's a balancing act, to be sure. When the audience is entertained and when the writers are able to show their work in its best light, I know I've done my job well. Here are some of the things I learned:

WHAT TO DO FOR YOUR READERS

Communicate clearly and often. If you're organizing the event, you'll often need to communicate the details to the readers (and later, to the audience). Not every writer is good with details, so you'll have to be. Communicate time, date, location, and your expectations for your participants clearly. Remind participants at least twice before the event. Confirm their attendance. Invite their questions. Be available to answer them.

Manage time—yours and theirs. As host of a readers' series or moderator of a panel, one of your primary jobs is managing time. It sometimes feels like trying to herd gnats getting a lot of writers and poets to be punctual, but it's important. I suggest urging your readers to arrive at least thirty minutes prior to the start of an event. It doesn't always work, but I'm clear and insistent on this matter. I also start the event on time, or at least I take the mike on time and let the audience know that we'll be starting very shortly if there's been some uncontrollable delay.

As host, it's also your job to keep the event moving, not allowing one panel member to dominate and eat up the time of the others. It's not about being a control freak—it's about respecting the event, the participants, and the audience.

When moderating a panel, I also make sure to balance the interaction rather than letting the most extroverted panelist dominate. To do so, I simply address a less vocal panelist by name. For example, I might say, *For the next question, let me start with Ava...* Or, *I'm especially curious, Mike, about your response to this given the content of your story.*

Be accessible. It's wise to share your cell number and to gather them from your readers for the just-in-case scenario the day of the event, or in the days or weeks prior to the event. People get lost, get ill, and have a host of other mishaps at the last minute. I just hate starting an event not knowing if an absent participant is just running late or if something more serious has occurred. Urge your guests to have cell phones on an hour before the event . . . just in case.

Set your participants up for success. If you're a panel moderator, it's good to give your guests an idea of the kinds of questions or topics you'll be using to facilitate the event. Ask open questions, giving them a chance to show their skill, knowledge, and wit. At writers events, these are not typically like journalistic interviews where you're trying to expose your guest's foibles or falsehoods or unearth their secrets.

If the content or mood on a panel gets too heavy, too tangential, or too silly, it's the moderator who has to put it back on track. A bit of humor, a reminder of the theme, or introducing a new question or topic can help change the mood and make topic transitions smoother. I like to think that it's my job as a moderator to be tuned in to the "temperature" of the room and keep it from getting too cold, or too hot.

If you're hosting a reading series, let your readers know what kinds of selections tend to work best for your audience, and which don't. Cue them about the venue details—everything from parking to microphone use—so that they know what to expect.

Warm the spot for each speaker. As host, it's your job to introduce the event as well as to introduce each speaker. Perhaps you'll read a short bio provided by your guests or, if you know them well, you might prepare one yourself.

When introducing the event, your job is to settle the room, set the tone, and warm up the crowd. You are the one to thank the venue host or the conference coordinator and to be the "salesman from the podium" if the readers are selling/signing books after. That does not necessarily mean that you are the one to collect the cash—that depends on the event.

WHAT TO DO FOR YOUR AUDIENCE

Take care of logistics. As part of introducing the event, let your audience know about the relevant logistics: where the restrooms are, whether there'll be an intermission, what the program is, the length of program, and so on. It's also your job to remind guests (including your readers and yourself) to silence cell phones, or invite them to "live post" the event on social media, if you'd like. To make triple sure that it's not my phone that goes off, I "demo" switching off the phone as I invite my audience to do so. This is wisdom born of pain, believe me. You'll make sure programs are distributed (if there is a program), chairs are set up, music in the environment is turned off, microphone(s) works, and the temperature of the room is within reason. Hosts should arrive early enough to correct any logistical problems.

Plan an audience-focused program. When arranging the order of readers or speakers, it's a good idea ask them about the general tone and content of what they intend to read or talk about and then set the program with the audience in mind. Three stories about dogs dying at the same event, for instance, would be absurd (unless the whole event is devoted to pet death, of course), so I may ask for one or more participant to choose another selection. Do this well in advance so your readers have time to prepare something else. Asking participants if their tone is dramatic, dark, funny, and so on helps you set the tone of the program.

I like to design programs to start and end with a strong reader or speaker. Some events are "all pro," where every reader is skilled, experienced, and known to the host. Others welcome newer voices, which may or may not be as strong. (And not every experienced writer is a fabulous reader.) A less skilled guest in the middle of the pack doesn't have as big a negative impact on the program overall as she might in the starting or closing spot.

Some writers have a bit of ego about where they read or speak in a program. Frankly, I haven't any room for this. I assure anyone I invite to an event that everyone is my guest and that I'll be designing the program with the audience in mind. If I have a guest of some renown, whom I know to be a WOW of a reader, I'll likely place him last in the program because it serves the program and the audience well, not because he's better known. You'd be surprised how many writers get nutty about "billing" and reading order though.

Depending upon the theme of the event, I'll often choose to end on a lighter note rather than a dark story. Whatever the case, I like to set the order of readers to make for a robust program that will be of value and entertaining to the audience.

Consider adding special touches. Acting as host is hard work and an honor. If you're in charge of the event, you may want to add your special touches to make it personal. Possibilities include having a vase of flowers at the front, offering beverages or nibbles, or giving tokens of appreciation to guest writers. Don't go crazy with this, stress out over it, or let little touches overshadow the event itself.

Don't insult your host bookstore. If your event is in a bookstore (whether you're a reader or the host) urging patrons to go onto Amazon to buy books is just plain rude. So many readers and hosts do this that it's become a pet peeve. Amazon, while most writers benefit from selling there, is in direct competition with bookstores. If members of your audience read only eBooks, they know how to access online sellers. No need to mention it. I treat this with respect and playfulness, urging bookstore audiences to support their local indie shops by buying their books there, but then go online to the "big online seller whose name I will not speak" to offer reviews. I consider Amazon (or the name of any other competitor of the bookstore that's acting as my host) the "Voldemort" of words. These are simply not to be uttered in a bookstore. With a playful tone and a wink, you can invite reviews and not insult your host.

Close the event with gratitude. Expressing appreciation for the guests, the venue host, the wait staff (if you're at an eatery), and the audience is a gracious ending to an event. Urge listeners to tip servers in eateries, to patronize the establishment, or to support the event and the art form at future events.

Most importantly, remember that it's not about you. Hosts that dominate the time with too much about themselves, their books, or otherwise showing off do not serve themselves or the event well. It's fine to ever-so-briefly mention that your book is on sale with the others. It's fine to play and be a pleasant part of the program. But that's it. Add your personality, of course, but don't try to be the star. Keep your own mike time confined. The guests are the feature, not you.

Tips for Making Introductions

Making introductions is another application of delivering content. Whether you're introducing a single speaker, acting as a panel moderator, or hosting a reading series with multiple readers, it's good to operate with a few principles and practices in mind.

- **Read and practice bios ahead of time.** Make sure you know how to pronounce everything in the bio, particularly the guest's name. Write it phonetically if it's tricky and ask for confirmation that you're saying it right *before* the event.
- **Shorten bios if needed.** A bio as intro is not a curriculum vitae. If you have multiple readers, shorter is better. You can ask readers to shorten their bios, or you can tell them that you'll have to.
- **Warm them up.** Some bios read cold. Either add a brief, but warm (or humorous) sentiment to a clinical sounding bio, or ask your featured speaker to do so. You can also go to their website or social media to gather a fun or fascinating tidbit to add.
- **Glow.** Of course, intros are complimentary and occasionally a guest is too modest in what they say about themselves in a written bio. Brag. Glow. Compliment. As long as it's warranted and sincere, it's your job to lay it on a bit.
- **Hawk the books.** If you reassure your guests that you will be the one to urge audience members to buy books, they won't have to do so during their reading time. As you open the event you can let listeners know that sales will happen after. If you're playful about it, it's much more fun than doing a hard sell. Remind listeners at the close about buying books.

As much as my introverted writer self hates to admit it, being in front of audiences is an important part of every author's platform of visibility. Reading your work at events and participating as part of a panel on topics relevant to your writing are both opportunities to gain visibility. Hosting such events and serving as a panel moderator to celebrate other writers is not only a great way to gain visibility, but an opportunity to support fellow writers and the art form we all hold dear.

I invite you to look more closely at hosts, moderators, and those making introductions by utilizing some of the Make It Stick suggestions below. By first observing, then welcoming opportunities like these, I'm confident that you'll find that they'll help you grow as a speaker. For me, these kinds of events have also proved to be soul-feeding, exposing me to other writers and their ideas. I've grown as a writer, as a speaker, and indeed, as a person by celebrating others. I hope you will, too.

Make It Stick

EXERCISE #1: LISTEN AGAIN, IN A NEW WAY

In previous Make It Stick segments (and those listed in the Bonus Track section of this book), I suggest many shows and podcasts that feature writers. By now, you've likely found ones that you enjoy. I invite you here to listen again to one that you enjoyed, but this time, pay special attention to the hosts. Take notice of their way of introducing their guest authors.

EXERCISE #2: SHOW UP

Here I invite you to be an audience member for live events that feature writers as readers or as panelists on a given topic. Many of these are free events.

- Check out your local coffee house, library, or community center and ask about such events.
- Writers' organizations are another great place to attend such readings or panel discussions. Whatever your genre, I suggest you find the writers' organizations that fit what you do. Some are large, national organizations: Romance Writers of America, The National Association of Memoir Writers (an online organization), Sisters in Crime, and many more. Not only do these organizations provide support, encouragement, and information to their members, they also offer opportunities to speak, read, and promote your work. Fees typically run under $200 a year, sometimes significantly

less than that for smaller, local organizations. Most such organizations allow you to visit as a guest for a meeting or two. You can kick the tires a bit and find the club that's right for you.

- Smaller writers' conferences can be local and conservatively priced. Larger, or national conferences can get pricey, of course. Still, these can be worthwhile investments for developing your craft and for meeting other writers and accomplished authors. If cost is an issue, offer to volunteer at conferences. Volunteers usually have time between their commitments to attend portions of the conference for free. This has allowed me to attend several high-end conferences when my budget was tight. I volunteered for two years at the San Francisco Writers Conference, the first time just as my debut novel was about to launch. Two years later, I was a speaker at that same conference.

I invite you to watch and listen to hosts and emcees as well as introductions closely at every event you attend. Whether broadcast or live, for entertainment or education, observe how hosts (skilled or unskilled) influence the quality of an event. See what you like and what you don't in a host.

CHAPTER 24

Pitches and Parties:
Tips for Speaking Well in Casual Conversation

"I'm trying to elevate small talk to medium talk."
—Larry David, comedy writer

Previous chapters focus on writer talks and readings. Frequently opportunities for us to talk about our writing arrive in the form of personal conversations, either one-on-one or with a few people, either in our casual encounters or when we're pitching our book ideas to agents or publishing professionals. We don't want to pushily pass out our cards like we're dealing Black Jack to uninterested party guests, though I now always have my cards in my pocketbook or tucked into my conference name tag pocket. The truth is that writers and their stories fascinate people and they often ask about our writing. Chance or arranged encounters where we're asked to talk about our books are yet another kind of public speaking opportunity. I'll offer a few tips to make these encounters easier:

Be Proud of Your Writing!

"Be careful how you're talking about yourself because people are listening."
—Lisa M. Hays, founder of Loving Yourself University

Here's where I'll confess another of my biggest pet peeves. As much as someone who brags can be annoying, I more often find that writers speak in such self-deprecating ways about themselves and their writing that it makes me want to walk out of the room. Whether you've never been published or you're on your tenth book, writing is an accomplishment. If you don't like what you've written and can't speak well of it, no one else will like it either.

If someone asks about what I write at a writers' conference or a social gathering, I express pride in the story. I'm not talking about bragging here, just feeling that my story is of value and worth reading. I hear things like this: *Oh, I'm just a dabbler. I've just written a little self-published book, it's not a bestseller or anything.* If you find yourself saying the word "just" a lot, as you describe you're writing, you are not representing your book well. It's fine to be honest. *I chose to self-publish the book. It's great to have cover-to-cover control because I love the story.*

See how different that is? Take pride.

Don't confuse self-deprecation with humility. Being humble, grateful, and admitting that you're new to the work are utterly different than talking yourself or your work down.

Have a Short Version of Your Story on the Tip of Your Tongue

Some people call this the "elevator pitch," a thirty-second or one-minute description of your story. If someone asks what you write, it's good to have a quick story to tell about it. Here's one of mine:

> *I've written a book called* Filling Her Shoes: A Memoir of an Inherited Family. *I married a widower with a young son and became the second mother to a boy whose mom was taken too soon. It's a sweet-bitter, happy-ending story of how love and loss aren't opposites, but cohabitants in every family's life.*

Notice how my short talk describes the theme of the book and a bit about the story, but not a bunch of details or names to forget. It took a bit of practice and I wrote (yes, wrote) several versions of this before I got it right and into an easily talkable form. When someone asks a writer about her book, I often hear her give a detailed and complex synopsis of the book that takes ten minutes. You can practically see people's eyes glaze over when you do this.

I prefer to offer a small bit, and if someone is genuinely interested, we converse and I offer a bit more detail. Remember, if this is conference chat with another writer, it's only polite to ask about what he's written as well. After you've said this elevator pitch a half a dozen times, it'll feel natural and won't sound canned. Try it on family member and pals, hone it, whittle it down, and get it comfortable before taking it out on the road.

Accept a Compliment

Non-writers are often impressed by writers. (As well they should be, in my opinion. I love writers, too!) If a conversation leads to a compliment, like, *Gosh, that's a beautiful cover*, or *I'm so impressed, I could never sit down to write a whole book*, don't kill the compliment. Writers, sadly, sometimes respond to such praise by saying, *It's not quite the cover I'd wanted, but . . .*, or *It's not that impressive to write a book—there are hundreds of thousands of new books a year*.

I would never buy or read a book if the author says such things about it. You don't have to brag, but it's fine to say, *Thanks a lot. I like the cover, too*. Or, *Writing is a lot of work and it's exciting to have a finished book*.

Carry Collateral Materials, Just in Case

Having business cards or bookmarks in your wallet or pocketbook is always a good idea. When someone is genuinely interested in your story, he may end up being a buyer, but may not recall your name or your book's title. It's polite to ask if your conversation buddy would like a card, of course, rather than pushing an unwanted card into someone's hands. I often buy books after I've met the author, have a pleasant exchange, and walk away with a card or a bookmark.

Remember That Agents Are People Too

Most large writers' conferences offer opportunities to pitch your book ideas to agents, editors, and publishers. It's a special opportunity to have such access. Time is often limited, sometimes as little as three or five minutes. Some conferences even call it "speed dating."

Many writers at conferences sit down at a pitch table nervous, and so worried about time that they launch right into their pitch without so much as a hello. Remember, the pros at these tables have likely gotten an earful before you arrive, maybe even a dozen earfuls. Take a moment to greet them, thank them for their time, and connect before you pitch. It's worth one of your five minutes to make a human connection. Give them your super-short synopsis (as described above) and a little more. Mention your genre, the title of your book, and why you are the perfect person to have written it. Then be quiet. Let them ask questions. It's a conversation, not a monologue, and you want it to be. After all, you're assessing them, too. You're seeing if this is a person with whom you want to work, while they're deciding if yours is work they want to represent. Make eye contact. Bring your sense of humor. Be proud, but don't brag. Be humble, but not self-deprecating. Practice with a pal beforehand.

Make sure you're pitching to an agent interested in the kind of writing you do. If you write sci-fi and you pitch to an agent who prefers religious material, you're wasting his time and yours.

And please . . . do *not* pitch publishing pros in the restroom. Honestly, I've seen this at least a dozen times at various conferences and have heard agents and editors complain about it. Tacky doesn't begin to describe.

Whether in casual encounters at dinner parties, at a table with fellow wordslingers at a writers' conference, or in a hopeful pitch to an agent or editor, talking about our writing in a more casual, conversational way is our most frequent public speaking opportunity. Writers comfortable with talking about their books in these encounters increase their odds for publication and commercial success. It's worth the practice.

CHAPTER 25

The Extra Extras: Food, Music, and Causes

There are times when adding the unexpected can take a presentation or an event to another level. None of the ideas in this chapter are required, but some of them are big fun. I call them the "extra extras." I would never want a speaker I coach to focus on these and forget the purpose for her being at an event, but extras can sometimes offer memorable moments that keep people talking after the event is long over, or they can add that personal touch that makes the event truly your own. I offer the following list of examples I've seen (or done) at book events and speaking gigs to get your juices flowing.

Food and Drink

If I serve food, I keep it easy. One or two items are plenty. I have hauled uneaten food home too many times. It's expensive and a pain.

Sometimes a book event can include a specific food is part of the theme of the event. Laurie McAndish King writes offbeat, delightfully irreverent travel stories of her adventures (and misadventures) on the road. When she launched *Lost, Kidnapped, Eaten Alive!*, Laurie offered a unique beverage to her guests, one that she'd written about in one of her travel tales: luwak coffee. For those unfamiliar, the beans of this coffee have been ingested, digested, and—*ahem*—evacuated by a small animal indigenous to Indonesia called *luwaks*, or Asian palm civets. (If you've seen the movie, "As Good as It Gets" starring Jack Nickolson and Helen Hunt, you'll recall his character's obsession with luwak coffee.) The coffee is part of just one of the travel stories in her collection. Laurie offered luwak coffee for the more adventurous guests. The coffee got everyone talking before the event. So much fun. What does luwak coffee taste like, you wonder? It tastes like coffee.

Judith Newton wrote a cozy mystery called *Oink* in which there's a murder committed by means of poisoned cornbread. She served homemade cornbread at her launch, minus the poison, of course.

Amy Peele, whom I mentioned for her transplant mystery in an earlier chapter, also wrote a memoir called *Aunt Mary's Guide to Raising Children the Old-Fashioned Way*. It's a nostalgic story of her childhood, and one of the chapters is called "Penny Candy." Amy provided a huge bowl full of the penny candies familiar to those of us who grew up in the middle of the century: root beer barrels, atomic fire balls, Pixie Sticks. It made everybody feel like a kid.

I share these stories not because you'll serve luwak coffee, cornbread, or penny candy, but as an inspiration to get creative. Is there a food or beverage that's predominant in your novel that would be fun and easy to share? If so, it can add a fun element to your event.

Music

Some reading events lend themselves to having music before, after, or as part of the event. This is especially valuable if you've written a book where music or musicians are a theme.

The downside is that music can be a hassle to include because of equipment acquisition, and sound intrusion if the space is public. If you keep it simple and check with your venue provider, it can add a wonderful sensory element to an event.

The incomparable Coleman Barks, known for his English translation and artful delivery of the poems by Rumi often performs with musicians playing as introduction and background to the poetry. Harp, tablas, sitar, and other instrumentation by talented musicians adds a dimension to his reading that is extraordinary. His audio books are some of my favorites.

Personal Extras

Many years ago, I attended a book launch of a longtime favorite author of mine, Elizabeth Berg. She was every bit as wonderful as I'd hoped a favorite author would be: warm, personal, and unpretentious. She also talked about one of the big hazards of her writing life as being "writers' spread," acquired from the sitting we do to create our art. She brought copies of her favorite Weight Watchers recipes to share with her audience. It was both charming and memorable and endeared me to her for life.

Pam Houston is one of my personal author idols. Nearly all her books and stories feature animals as characters, particularly her beloved Irish wolfhounds. I am fortunate to have attended several of her events, and most memorable among them was when she brought William, her dignified (and *huge*) hound, who rested comfortably on the floor beside her as she spoke and offered sniffs and snuggles to visitors afterward. It has to be the right animal and okayed by your venue, of course. But come on, who can resist a great dog?

Julie Barton, whom I also mentioned earlier as the author of *Dog Medicine*, gave custom-made dog biscuits at her book launch. (My dog Edgar loved his.)

Occasionally at a book launch, I've seen authors offer a printed list of her favorite books and authors, with her contact information at the bottom. I love learning what people are reading and this is a nice way to pay homage to our writer heroes and to promote the reading of great books. This costs nothing but a bit of time and the cost of paper. Plus, I like the idea of championing the work of others. Consider it good book karma.

Drawings and Prizes

At events where I'm the host, workshop leader, or those where I'm the featured speaker, I circulate a sign-up sheet requesting email addresses. This adds to my contact list, which has proven to be a valuable tool for promoting my writing events and books. When I ask people to sign the sheet, I often offer an incentive. I'll pick a random name from the list and give a free book or audio book of mine, a bottle of wine, or some other item apropos to the event. This technique of gathering names is sometimes called a "bribe to subscribe." It's fun. It works. And people love it.

Fundraisers

Some writers' events also serve as fundraisers. Sometimes the author or authors reading donate a percent of their book sales to a cause. Sometimes there's a modest door fee and that funds the project. This can be both an exceptional way to support a cause that you hold dear and a way to gain some publicity for your event. Local newspapers are more likely to feature fundraisers than common book launches or readings.

One note of caution: Choosing a cause that is highly controversial or with a particular political slant can limit your audience. If you're fine with that and your cause is important enough to you, go for it. By the same token, that very same cause may draw an audience skewed toward your values and views, which may mean that your audience is populated with those more aligned with your book or ideas. Either way, consider the value to your cause, to your event, and to your audience.

Trinkets, Bookmarks, and More

There is no shortage of opportunity to purchase customized bling for the purposes of book promotion. Bookmarks, pens, and other trinkets (aka *collateral material*) adorned with your book's cover can be nice giveaways at events where you're featured, or handy promotional tools if you're manning a booth at a book fair or a similar event.

Some publishers provide such materials, but most don't and it's the author's out-of-pocket expense. Online sources and local print shops offer a multitude of design and printing options for such materials, as do your local print shops and larger office supply stores. Cards and bookmarks are worth the investment, in my experience. The rest is optional. It's worth some coin to have support materials, but do be thoughtful about it. Having too many different kinds of toys can get pricey, it's a lot of stuff to lug around, and you may not find them all useful.

Conclusion for Part 5

The largest portion of this book is devoted to the most essential elements of getting writers ready for public speaking. Beyond the essentials, it's fun to add a little sparkle to an event. While these sparkles should never occupy so much of our energy and time that we don't have time to prepare and practice our talks, it is the bling that often adds an element of fun to an event, and *fun* is memorable.

Observe other writers, their events, and their resources. Feel free to embellish your writer events by infusing creativity and your own playful or dramatic visual elements. And remember that whenever you're talking about your writing—whether it's to an audience of one or a roomful—you *are* public speaking.

Make It Stick

I have a challenge to you as you consider being a part of, or hosting, writer events. In the words of the Nike company: *Just do it.* Don't wait for confidence to arrive. Start doing events that help you gain confidence. Here are some exercises.

EXERCISE #1: FIRST, ATTEND WRITER EVENTS

Ask your local librarians and booksellers if they know of any existing writing organizations. Find one that fits you and attend. Often writers' organizations host reading events or know of them. This is a good place to find local events you don't already know about.

Find independent reading salons, poetry slams, and other places near you. Then go! Go to support other writers. Go to learn what skills look and sound like. Go to shop for which events might be a fit for you to read your work.

EXERCISE #2: THEN, APPLY TO READ

After you've attended an event for a bit, find out what their requirements are for reading. See if they welcome work like yours. Apply. Even if they don't accept you, keep attending (assuming you enjoy that particular event) and go to others that may be a better fit for your work.

EXERCISE #3: RECORD YOURSELF

If you're not comfortable reading in public, try reading for yourself first. By recording your voice, you'll get a better "read" on how you read. Experiment. Try to be extreme with your vocal animation and see how it sounds on the recording.

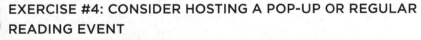

EXERCISE #4: CONSIDER HOSTING A POP-UP OR REGULAR READING EVENT

If there's not much around you as far as reading series go, try hosting one. Often coffee houses, libraries, and some restaurants will let you use the space for free or for a nominal fee. Social media is free advertising. If you have three to six readers who invite their friends, you're sure to have an audience of at least ten to fifteen people, and more over time if you make it a regular affair and it gets a good reputation.

My events were free to the public for years and I loved being able to do that. As the event grew, I had to rent chairs and space and it got a little pricey. I started requesting a $10 donation at the door, $5 for students, and I included in the announcement and with a sign at the door that if the entry fee was a hardship, everyone was welcome to attend for free, and should feel guilt-free as long as they applauded extra loudly. I made enough money to cover expenses and keep the series going for years.

EXERCISE #5: CONTINUE TO LISTEN TO PODCASTS AND PROGRAMS IN WHICH AUTHORS READ

The resource section at the end of this book includes a few of these. Ask friends, ask librarians, do an Internet search, and you're bound to find many writers reading stories, serials, and poetry, as well as talking craft. Audio books are another great option.

The main point is to keep learning. Keep growing. Keep taking risks.

Wrapping it up:
My Big Message to Fellow Writers

In addition to providing information about the rationale for, and techniques of, public speaking, my intention with this book is to provide you with encouragement. In my life as a therapist, as a writer, and as a coach to writers and speakers, I have come to define this as one of my purposes in life: to empower the voices of others in their intimate conversations, their written stories, and when they're speaking to audiences of any size about the topics and ideas they hold dear.

This world is a richer, kinder, more compassionate place because of the storytellers of this world. Whatever your genre, whatever your style, I hope that you've gained a nugget—or maybe twelve—to help you gain the courage and the skill to find your strongest, most confident, and authentic speaking voice to augment the squiggles that you make on a page. It's magic turning ink into stories. It's another kind of magic to turn thin air and breath into stories that captivate listeners. I hope you've gained a bit of information and enough inspiration to move your words from ink to air . . . from the page to the stage.

The world needs your utterly unique voice.

Acknowledgments

I owe a unique debt of gratitude to Linda High, without whom I'd never have voluntarily stood in front of a group of people to speak. By urging me to take—no, shoving me into—my first public speaking class twenty years ago, Linda single-handedly changed the course of my life, opening the possibility for me to publish books, teach and coach others, and speak out about the causes and issues I hold dear. Friend. Sister. Inspiration. Everybody needs a sister-friend like Linda.

I have had the honor of working with, for, and around several communications training companies. To the colleagues who have coached me, inspired me, taught me tricks, and shared their generous hearts, I thank you. Clients have trusted me to coach them in their most vulnerable moments, I am honored and inspired by them all.

She Writes Press now feels less like my publisher, and more like my community. Brooke Warner, Crystal Patriarche, and the whole SWP team and the authors who are theSWP sisterhood, you deserve more than these inky appreciations. I was never a sorority girl, but I sure am grateful to be a part of this one. Cait Levin, thanks for your gentle nudges and Tabitha Lahr, special gratitude for a beautiful cover and graphics designs.

Joan Keyes, your mad skills and generous spirit pulled me from the brink on this book. I'll be forever steeped in gratitude for your friendship. Catherine Marshall-Smith, thank you for allowing me to use the preparations we did for the launch of your beautiful book as an example in this one. I'm holding out hope that you'll live closer one day soon. We have some serious hanging out to do.

Whether it is by fate or choice or happy accident, I have been given partners in my writing life the value of whom is immeasurable. Linda Joy Myers, Christie Nelson, and Amy Peele, you are more than partners, more than friends, you are family. Gratitude abounds for your many touches on my work and on my life.

My family (Grubbs, Shells, Fasbinders, Lundgrens, Wrens, and soon-to-be Chao)is so whole-heartedly supportive of my every endeavor. I am infinitely fortunate. For bringing a glass of wine to my studio at five, picking up supper, planting calla lilies outside of my studio window, and for a million other acts of support, Tom Fasbinder . . . you have my heart. I promise we can go on Sunday drives again, now that this book is done.

Resources and References

I love hearing from readers. Find me at:

Betsy Graziani Fasbinder, website at www.betsygrazianifasbinder.com

@BetsyGFasbinder

BetsyGFAuthor

betsygrazianifasbinder

WriterBGF

Given the transient nature of websites and links and the more permanent nature of books, I've listed the titles of these resources rather than links. They're easily found with a simple search with Google or your preferred search engine.

INVITATION:

Information on Toastmasters is available at Toastmasters.com

"Saying Yes! To Your Weirdness," TED Talk by J.D. Sears

"The Beauty of Being a Misfit," TED Talk by Lidia Yiknavitch

PART 1

What's Your Book: A Step-by-Step Guide to Get You from Inspiration to Published Author, by Brooke Warner

"Green-Light Revolution," TEDx Talk by Brooke Warner

Making your Mind Magnificent by Steven R. Campbell, and his website at stevenrcampbell.com

PART 2

Writing Blockbuster Plots: A Step-by-Step Guide to Mastering Plot, Structure, and Scene, by Martha Alderson

The Plot Whisperer: Secrets of Story Structure Any Wrier Can Master, by Martha Alderson

Also check out Martha Alderson's YouTube station, where she offers free plot coaching videos that are both informative for writers and a demonstration of another kind of author speaking opportunity.

Hooked: Write Fiction That Grabs Readers at Page One and Never Lets Them Go, by Les Edgerton

Tools of the Writer's Craft, by Sands Hall

American Family, by Catherine Marshall-Smith

The Pyramid Principle, by Barbara Minto

The Hero's Journey, by Joseph Campbell

"Plus Size, How About My Size?" TED Talk by Ashley Graham

Shonda Rhimes, Dartmouth Commencement Address, 2015

Neil deGrasse Tyson has many YouTube videos; try a few.

PART 3

"Your Body Language May Shape Who You Are," TED Talk by Amy Cuddy

Search Oprah Winfrey's first national "Oprah" show.

Marilyn Maye, *CBS Sunday Morning*

David Sedaris reading "The Incomplete Quad" on YouTube

David Whyte reading "The Journey" on YouTube

"On Genius," TED Talk by Elizabeth Gilbert

Podcast: "Magic Lessons" by Elizabeth Gilbert

Audiobook: *The Poisonwood Bible,* by Barbara Kingsolver

Podcast: National Public Radio's "This American Life"

Podcast: National Public Radio, "Fresh Air"

"The Power of Introverts", TED Talk by Susan Cain

PART 4

The Four Agreements, by Don Miguel Ruiz

Lauren Conrad on "Sway in the Morning"

"Super Soul Sunday," hosted by Oprah Winfrey

Podcast: Sherman Alexie on "Fresh Air"

Podcast: Greta Gerwig on Fresh Air

Podcast: "Ten Minute Writer's Workshop"

Podcast: "The Newbie Writers Podcast", Hosted by Damien Bloth and Catherine Bramkamp

National Association of Memoir Writers (NAMW), hosted by Linda Joy Myers. This is both a writers' association and a resource for hearing author and industry expert interviews. Many of the classes are offered for free or at great discount to NAMW members for a nominal annual fee.

"Shark Tank", ABC-TV show

PART 5

"A Special Beast: Giving Readings That Work" by Gabriel Cohen, in *The Practical Writer*, September/October, 2008

Lost, Kidnapped, Eaten Alive! by Laurie McAndish King

Cut, by Amy S. Peele

Dog Medicine, by Julie Barton

Bamboo Secrets, by Patricia Dove Miller

Beautiful Illusion, by Christie Nelson

About the Author

Betsy Graziani Fasbinder is an award-winning author, a licensed psychotherapist, and an in-demand communications trainer. She has coached public speaking for the reluctant and the downright phobic in fortune 500 companies throughout the US and abroad. She coaches others to conquer their stage fears, connect to listeners, and never again allow a fear of public speaking to be an obstacle. She is the author of *Fire & Water* and *Filling Her Shoes: A Memoir of an Inherited Family*. Betsy and her husband live in their recently empty nest north of San Francisco with their beloved blind old dog Edgar Alan Paw, who continues to teach them new kinds of unconditional love and acceptance.

Author photo © Chris Loomis

Selected Titles From She Writes Press

She Writes Press is an independent publishing company founded to serve women writers everywhere. Visit us at www.shewritespress.com.

Green-Light Your Book: How Writers Can Succeed in the New Era of Publishing by Brooke Warner. $16.95, 978-1-63152-802-6. A straight-shooting guide to a changing industry that gives indie publishers and authors insight into the current state of publishing, as well as the tools they need to make their books a smashing success.

The Art of Play: Igniting Your Imagination to Unlock Insight, Healing, and Joy by Joan Stanford. $19.95, 978-1-63152-030-3. Lifelong "non-artist" Joan Stanford shares the creative process that led her to insight and healing, and shares ways for others to do the same.

This Way Up: Seven Tools for Unleashing Your Creative Self and Transforming Your Life by Patti Clark. $16.95, 978-1-63152-028-0. A story of healing for women who yearn to lead a fuller life, accompanied by a workbook designed to help readers work through personal challenges, discover new inspiration, and harness their creative power.

Breaking Ground on Your Memoir by Linda Joy Myers and Brooke Warner. $14.95, 978-1-631520-85-3. Myers and Warner present from the ground up—from basic to advanced—the craft and skills memoirists can draw upon to write a powerful and moving story, as well as inspiration to write, finish, and polish their own story.

Journey of Memoir: The Three Stages of Memoir Writing by Linda Joy Myers. $22.95, 978-1-938314-26-1. A straightforward, highly effective workbook designed to help memoirists of every level get their story on the page.

Think Better. Live Better. 5 Steps to Create the Life You Deserve by Francine Huss. $16.95, 978-1-938314-66-7. With the help of this guide, readers will learn to cultivate more creative thoughts, realign their mindset, and gain a new perspective on life.

CPSIA information can be obtained
at www.ICGtesting.com
Printed in the USA
BVHW07s1924210918
527810BV00003B/6/P

9 781631 524639